KATIE'S WAR

—— A STORY OF THE IRISH CIVIL WAR ——

'Very, very impressive indeed'
Robert Dunbar, The Gay Byrne Show

'the writing is resonant and strong ... the gripping climax is compelling reading'
CHILDREN'S BOOKS IN IRELAND

'a dramatic book, full of history and action ...
10 out of 10'
A child's review, THE WICKLOW PEOPLE

Special Merit Award to The O'Brien Press
from Reading Association of Ireland
*'for exceptional care, skill and professionalism in
publishing, resulting in a consistently high standard in all
of the children's books published by The O'Brien Press'*

AUBREY FLEGG

Aubrey Flegg was born in Dublin. His early childhood was spent in County Sligo. He went to school in Dublin and later in England. After a spell with a mountain rescue team in Scotland, he returned to Ireland to study geology at Trinity College. He then did geological research in Kenya, before joining the Geological Survey of Ireland in 1968. *Katie's War* is his first book and it won the Peter Pan Award 2000 – an award created by IBbY Sweden for a children's book, translated into Swedish, which gives information on another culture. *Katie's War* has also been translated into German. Aubrey's second book, *The Cinnamon Tree*, deals with the issue of landmines and the international arms trade, and it was listed in the White Ravens selection for 2001.

KATIE'S WAR

Aubrey Flegg

THE O'BRIEN PRESS
DUBLIN

First published 1997 by The O'Brien Press Ltd.,
20 Victoria Road, Rathgar, Dublin 6, Ireland.
Tel: +353 1 4923333; Fax: +353 1 4922777
E-mail books@obrien.ie
Website www.obrien.ie
Reprinted 1998, 1999, 2001.

ISBN: 0-86278-525-1

British Library Cataloguing-in-Publication Data
Katie's war: a story of the Irish Civil War
1. Ireland - history - Civil War, 1922-1923 -
juvenile fiction 2. children's stories
I. Title
823.9'14 [J]

4 5 6 7 8 9 10
01 02 03 04 05

The O'Brien Press receives
assistance from the arts
council
an chomhairle
ealaíon
50

Typesetting, editing, layout, design: The O'Brien Press Ltd.
Cover separations: C&A Print Services Ltd.
Printing: Cox & Wyman Ltd.

DEDICATION

To Jennifer
and to the people of North Tipperary
whose hospitality we enjoyed for
three memorable years

ACKNOWLEDGEMENTS

I have received a lot of help during the writing of this book, chiefly with the history of the time. I must thank my mother, whose library of books and memories provided the core of my research. Pat Ryan of the *Nenagh Guardian* allowed me to leaf through his paper's precious archive of back numbers. My thanks to local historians: Michael Joy of Curragh, who lent me his detailed notes on the history of the slate country around Portroe, and Sean Kierse of Killaloe, who helped me particularly with aspects of Katie's education. Local historians must be the answer to the writer's prayer.

Gordon Herries Davies and Geoffrey Martin advised me on aspects of war in the trenches. Philip Smyly helped me with Dafydd's train journey through Dublin and also with a vivid personal memory of a Crossley Tender full of Black and Tans. Bobby Buckley helped me with the Latin Mass and Ms B. Davies of UCD kindly translated Dafydd's few words of Welsh for me. My thanks to all of these. Any inaccuracies or biases which may have crept in are entirely of my making.

Finally, my thanks to my wife Jennifer, who has supported my aspirations as a writer over many years of aspiration. And to Íde ní Laoghaire and all at the O'Brien Press, who have worked so hard to make a book out of a mere manuscript.

CONTENTS

CHAPTER 1

The Black Dogs

Katie knew she was dreaming. She even forced her eyes open for a moment. The grey light of an early summer morning filtered in at the window, but still the black dogs were after her. This was an old dream, a dream from her past. Why wouldn't the dogs leave her alone? Her eyes closed and the dream swirled around her like a fog

She stood ankle-deep in mud; a cold wind plucked at her frock. In the distance the sky flickered, and the grumble of great guns told her where 'some poor souls were getting a pasting'. She knew the dogs were there, moving silently through the trenches, stepping over dead men. She wanted the guns to stop. She might hear the dogs coming then, their panting perhaps, or the sucking noise of their paws in the mud.

At her feet a wounded soldier sat leaning against her knees. One hand had been shot away and the stump was crudely bandaged. The black dogs didn't want him for that, oh no, not for a mere wound. They wanted him for Katie's secret. They had guessed it – but they didn't know for sure. She could hear them taunting her.

'Give up your secret, Katie,' they howled. 'We know he's your father, we know about his hand too, but what about his mind, Katie? Go on! Admit it – he's mad, Katie – mad as a hatter.' A deep shudder passed through her. 'Shame can turn people mad you know ... go on, Katie, ask him why he ran away ...'

'No,' she whispered, forcing the sound out. Then loudly, 'NO!'

As if at her command the grumble of guns died away. The dogs disappeared. Light burst from the clouds to the east and fell on swathe after swathe of brilliant red poppies. She bent and helped her father to his feet and they walked home together through the poppies with the sun behind them.

*   *   *

When Katie woke, the grey of early morning had, as if by magic, given way to bright sunlight. It glanced across the lace curtains which stirred in the air at the window. For a moment she was tense. Why was she here? What about school? Then, with a tingle of relief, she remembered she was on holiday. Father had taken them out of school two days early as a protest at the leaks in the roof. On Friday, school would break up anyway for the longest summer holidays ever. Three whole months while the teachers went back to class themselves to learn Irish.

She lay on her back in bed and stretched out comfortably towards its four corners. A delicious feeling of peace and contentment swept over her. She smiled, thinking of her teacher. Poor Miss Kennedy – she had looked so worried. Not a word of Irish and she was going to have to teach it! She thought about her own future too. Father said that now the fighting was over she could go to the Sisters of Mercy Secondary School in Nenagh. It was only seven miles and she could cycle that easily. In winter she could board with her cousin Dolores. It would be fun to stay in a real town, and Dolores knew everyone. 'Secondary school!' she said to herself with satisfaction.

The homely sounds of the farmyard came up to her from below, along with the occasional clatter from the kitchen and the voice of her mother. Katie strained to hear who she was talking to. She could not distinguish any words, but the pitch of the voice was familiar. It was her elder brother Seamus. Her mother and Seamus were always talking; they would discuss politics, the war with the English, which was now over, thank God, and other things that Katie had put out of her mind since her father had come back from the war – the Great War, that is, that was fought in the trenches in France. Seamus was two years older than she and, at seventeen, should be helping run the farm, but it was her thirteen-year-old brother Marty who was the real farmer.

Seamus was always up to something. She must find out what he and Mother were scheming about now. She heard his voice rise angrily for a moment. Ever since Mr Collins had come back from London having signed a treaty with the English that Mr DeValera did not like, Mother and Seamus had sided with Mr DeValera, while Father held fast to Mr Collins. Perhaps, if she were going to secondary school, she should learn something about politics?

She could hear Marty now, talking to the cows, slapping their backsides as he drove them down from the byre. They could only milk three cows at a time in the byre, so they were brought in in two lots. Six cows is a good number; you're well off with six cows to milk. She closed her eyes and imagined Peter milking, cap down over his forehead, his head pressed against the cow's flank. Peter was the cowman, and the every-thing-else-man for that matter. The jets of milk would make a lively ping-ping in the pail to begin with, then as the pail filled, the sound would become rich and frothy.

Nailed boots scraped in the yard. That was Father – she could tell from the slight limp he still had from the war. The steel hook, which replaced the hand he had lost, clinked on the milk churn as he handled it out of the byre. With the comforting sun glancing through the curtains, Katie let her mind drift back to that dreadful time four years ago when Father had come back from the war. She was only eleven then.

* * *

She had gone with her mother to meet Father at the station in Nenagh. They all stepped back as the huge steam-engine hissed past, the driver leaning from the cab, the fire from the fire-box gleaming red on his face. It was winter, and clouds of steam blew up from between the carriages. Doors swung open and passengers climbed down, but there was no sign of Father. She turned to look up at Mother, who was standing on tiptoe searching for him in the crowd. Then Katie turned back, the steam parted, and there he was, standing in the throng of passengers and cases. He was wearing a cumbersome great-coat and his left arm was in a sling, the cuff pinned back over where his hand had been. She had been told about the hand; she was a big girl and was ready for it.

'Father!' Katie called, hurtling down the platform. She grabbed him about the waist and looked up at his face. But Father just stood there. He did not even look down. Amid the bustle and clatter and smell of hot steam she hugged him, gazing up, while he stared out over her head.

Mother came and kissed him, but he looked over her shoulder too towards something neither of them could see. When they compared notes later they told each other he had smiled, but that was just because it was what they wanted to believe. Then, like a blind man, he allowed them to lead him away.

For a whole year he did not speak, but ate his meals and then walked stiffly back to his place beside the range. Doing her homework with Marty at the kitchen table, while her mother mended or darned, Katie would look up from the pool of light cast by the lamp and try to penetrate the blackness around him.

Were those sunken, staring eyes looking at her? She would try not to think of them, but then she would imagine their glint in the darkness, pulling her towards him. She could not think of him as her father, not yet, but time and again her eyes rose and she found herself straining to see him in the dark corner of the room.

One day, pretending to be cold, she abandoned her place at the kitchen table and moved the little table, which was usually pushed back against the wall, over near where he sat.

'It's closer to the range,' she said, by way of explanation. She brought in a spare oil lamp and put it on the table beside her where it cast a safe glow of yellow light over the table and her work. She could see his hand out of the corner of her eye, but the dreadful staring face was hidden.

'Hurray!' said Marty. 'The mutter-machine has gone.'

'I don't mutter!' she protested.

'Here's me with both fingers in my ears till they meet in the middle, and she says she doesn't mutter.'

'They meet in the middle because there's nothing in between!' Katie answered.

'Now, children!' Mother intervened.

This place near her father became Katie's favourite position in the evenings. She read slowly in those days, pronouncing the words carefully; she liked words, almost as much as she hated numbers. She would rush at numbers, meeting them head-on, until in the end, they seemed to scatter over the slate she was working on like frightened chickens. And she *did* mutter. She would forget about Father a lot of the time now.

'Twelve hens at one shilling and sixpence each?' she read one evening. Then, calculating, 'So, twelve sixes are seventy-two, now divide by twelve, that's ... Oh! Lord help me, it's six again, but are these hens or shillings?' Tears of frustration trickled down her face. It was her third try at the sum. Suddenly, out of the darkness, her father's hand moved.

Very slowly, it came towards her, advancing into her pool of light. She watched, terrified but fascinated. Something momentous was happening. She wanted Mother to see, but her tongue seemed stuck to the top of her mouth. She could neither speak nor move. The hand touched her arm and she tried not to flinch. It was not cold, as she had imagined, but warm. It rested on her arm as lightly as her mother's silk scarf. She stared at it. Gradually her own right hand came over and rested for a moment on his. A sob rose from deep inside her. Her mother looked over. 'What's the matter, child?' But the hand had gone.

'It's these blessed sums,' lied Katie.

'Now, don't you swear! Leave the old sums till morning. It's time for bed.'

That was how it had started. From then on, as Katie worked, she recited her homework aloud for Father. No-one else noticed, but then, no-one listened to Katie's mutterings anyway. After a while she started telling him little bits about the day amongst her mutterings: about the funny things Marty had done, or which cow was calving. He still did not speak but gradually his face lost its dead look. Mother saw it first.

'Katie,' she said, 'I think you have a way with your father. Your mutterings seem to be doing him good. I can see him listening.'

Easter brought spring-cleaning and whitewashing. Even Father was evicted from the kitchen while the whitewash was applied. He and Katie sat among the primroses on a bank above the house.

'Beautiful,' he said.

That was all. His first word and Katie didn't even notice.

13

'I love primroses,' she said, then caught her breath. 'Father, you spoke!' Stopping only to give him a kiss, she rushed down to tell the others.

*   *   *

Katie lay back in bed smiling at the memory of that moment when Father had spoken. They had all congregated in the kitchen, Father looking pleased but dazed, and there among the buckets of whitewash they had an impromptu party of tea and soda bread; there was nothing else as it was Lent, but the tea went to their heads like wine. Katie was praised and hugged as if it was she, not Father, who had talked.

She was twelve that May. Come summer, it seemed obvious to everyone that Father was on the mend, and Katie felt that it was all her own work.

'Leave the washing now, child,' her mother would say. 'Take your father up by the slate quarries, he needs a breath of fresh air.' The sun shone and everyone seemed happy.

But quite suddenly, for Katie, it all changed.

*   *   *

Together Katie and Father explored the slate quarries and trod the roads and lanes for miles around. He followed where she led. He seldom spoke and her chatter seemed to wash over him. If she left him and went to pick flowers or ran ahead to hunt the devils from her legs because his slow walk could be tiresome, he would just stand where she had left him, often with a half-smile on his face. She would come back to him then and slip her hand into his, always her left hand into his right. His smile would widen like a blind man's when his keeper returns.

'Beautiful,' he would say, and the little squeeze he gave her hand would leave her wondering if it was the view, or the sunshine, or perhaps even she who was beautiful.

It happened first in early summer. The new-mown hay lay in silver ribbons in the fields. A piece of twisted metal, broken off from a mower, was thrown beside the road. Suddenly Father stopped and gripped Katie's arm. She looked up, surprised. To her horror she saw that his face had gone rigid and chords stood out on his neck. He was staring at the piece of metal, apparently addressing it.

'A hundred and sixty-four men you killed last night,' he said, low and menacingly. Then he shouted, 'Answer me, damn you!' Katie cried out as her father's fingers closed on her arm like steel. 'Who made you to kill and maim? These were *my* men, my body, my legs, my heart, torn apart by you!' This was more than he had ever said since coming home. There were flecks of foam at the corners of his mouth. Katie looked desperately up and down the road, torn between wanting help and hoping no-one would see. He turned to her, eyes piercing, demanding attention.

'You want to know why I ran?' he demanded. 'I'll tell you.' She wanted to cover her ears and scream. Even now she had to shut her mind to what he told her then because he talked of the unspeakable things of war – the stench of bodies, dying friends, and running – running. Eventually he stopped, exhausted. The madman's grip on her arm loosened. She gazed at him in horror, ready to run, but a puzzled half-quizzical smile came over his face.

'That's funny,' he said, his speech suddenly set free and his voice normal now. 'That bit of metal reminded me of the war.' He shook his head. 'Not for your ears, my child,' and gave her the gentlest squeeze with his good arm. They walked on. A stoat peered from a wall, and he pointed it out to her.

'Look at it's sharp little face, Katie,' he said.

But Katie's world was shaken. The ground which had seemed so firm under her feet only moments ago now seemed wobbly and uncertain, like a quaking bog.

'That bit of metal, Father ...?' she ventured tentatively.

'What?'

Katie was only inches away from him and looking up into his face, but she could swear that he had already forgotten about it.

'God love you, child. Just some old memories. Haven't you cured me of all that?'

She turned away and looked up the road. Two black dogs were trotting purposefully towards them. A shiver went down her spine though she had never been afraid of dogs.

'There's two fellows up to no good,' said Father. At the sound of his voice the dogs stopped, stared, and then turned away over the bank and vanished out of sight into the fields beyond. What had they heard? Katie wondered foolishly, peering in the direction they had gone.

To begin with, the attacks of madness or whatever it was were frequent, and always came when they were alone and far from home. Katie started having nightmares then, and the black dogs came into her dreams trying to hear what Father said. Her nightmares were not just about the horrors of war; there were dreams too in which men in white coats came to take her father away. Terrified that she would lose him, Katie told no-one, not even her mother. Was Father a madman? No one must know – ever! Gradually Father's attacks became less and less frequent; he even lost the habit of throwing back his head to ease the tightening muscles in his neck. There seemed to be no point in telling Mother then – he was better, and it was Katie who had cured him.

*　　*　　*

16

From her bed Katie listened to the whistling below in the yard and smiled. What on earth had got her dreaming of the black dogs again? Happily, that time was long over now. It was time to think of herself and of the summer ahead.

CHAPTER 2

The Handsome Soldier

'Katie, are you going to lie in bed all day?' Mother called from the yard, banging lustily on the basin of hen-feed as she called, '*Chook*, chook, chook, chook.'

Katie pulled up her knees, then shot her legs down again so that the sheet billowed out over the end of the bed. She swung her feet on to the rush mat beside her bed and cocked her head. She could hear the hens pecking on the corrugated iron sheet in the open cart-shed opposite; it sounded like rain on a tin roof. She got up, knelt on the window ledge and leant out. The top of her mother's head was just disappearing back into the house below. Late-comers among the hens were hurrying towards the shed, their necks stretched out. Marty was standing by the byre door. He looked up, saw Katie, and began an exaggerated yawning and rubbing-eyes routine. His bare feet were covered with muck.

'Wash your feet,' she called. He kicked one foot up and wiggled his toes at her. Then he pretended to try to lift the other leg, using both hands, and nearly fell over. Despite herself, Katie laughed and ducked back into the room. Against the wall by the door was a wash-stand. On it was a china basin with red painted roses, and a tall china jug that nearly matched. The soap dish was a saucer which she'd chosen because it also had roses on it. She leaned forward to look in the mirror. A broad freckled face, two blue eyes and an unruly mass of red hair looked back at her. The face was still smiling from Marty's antics, so she stuck her tongue out at it, then she dipped a hand into the water jug and gave two token dabs at her face, one on each cheek, and reached for the towel. She was just burying her face in it when she stopped. The visitors! She'd forgotten about the visitors. She wasn't sure whether her heart sank or not. It was a Welsh man, a friend of her father's from the war, coming to advise him about reopening their slate quarry. He was bringing his son – for the experience apparently. She wondered what he'd be like. She was fifteen; perhaps he'd be Seamus's age and working now?

To begin with she had been angry at the thought of having visitors at the beginning of the holidays. But now, rather to her surprise, she realised she was looking forward to the visit. She poured water from the jug into the basin. She imagined the boy in her mind. She'd never felt any real need for boys and most of the nicer ones had left school at fourteen. Anyway, she'd had Father to look after – perhaps the boys had kept away because he was always there. She wasn't going to start bothering about them now. Laughing at herself, she scooped water over her face and neck and washed thoroughly before taking her best frock from behind the curtain which closed off the press in the corner. She had a pleasant feeling of anticipation. Father had promised to take her with him when he went to collect the visitors in the horse and trap; a trip into Nenagh was special. She battled briefly with her hair until she could catch it at the back with a ribbon, then she poured the water from the basin into the enamel bucket under the wash-stand and ran downstairs.

'Oh Katie,' said her mother, seeing her dressed up, 'I should have said – the train will be late. The postman looked in to say there has been some trouble in Dublin. The train will not be in till twelve or later.' Katie hesitated, wondering if she should go back up and change. Then she noticed that her mother had stopped working the bread dough that was caking on her hands.

'What's the matter? What sort of trouble? You look worried, Mother.'

'I am worried ...' she hesitated, 'I think there may be fighting.'

'How can there be? Isn't the war against England over? We have Home Rule now, haven't we?'

'We have and we haven't, child. The sad fact of the matter is that we can't trust the English. For as long as we have to swear allegiance to their king they have us like a pig on a string, and that's how they think of us too. Any excuse and they'll take back what they've given, and they have the forces to do it too. We want them out of Ireland – all of Ireland – once and for all. I can see that treaty splitting us apart like a badly snagged turnip.'

'Well, it won't split our family, Mother,' said Katie, leaning forward, avoiding the doughy hands and kissing Mother on the cheek. 'I won't let it.'

'I hope you're right, chick. I hope you're right.' Mother placed the moist dough into a floured baking tin and slid it into the range. 'Well then. Your porridge is inside the pigs by now. Will you have an egg?'

* * *

Katie loved a ride in the trap. Since she was tiny she had liked the bounce of the springs and the feeling of being locked in once the little door at the back of the trap was closed. She used to think that she had only to say the right word and Barney, farm horse that he was, would spread wings and together they would fly out over the patchwork of fields of her beloved Tipperary. They would swoop down then and gallop so low over Lough Derg that his hooves would catch the blue wave-tops and the wheels would spin in the foam. Then they would rise up and fly over the little harbour of Garrykennedy and look down on the castle and the up-turned faces of the people unloading the turf that had come all the way from Galway in barges blown on brown sails. This morning Barney seemed to catch her enthusiasm and, for a while at any rate, they clipped along at a fine rate between the hedges, making for the main road.

Father had made a loop in the left rein for his hook, but the horse needed little guidance. They could see the line of the main road before they got to it from the white dust clinging to the hedges. The loose chippings had been recently rolled and the pot-holes filled in, so it felt almost as smooth as if driving on tar when they turned on to it. There was little traffic on the road, just a few carts, but Father kept a look out for the steam-roller. Father often said that Barney was too flighty for a farm horse and certainly, if Barney had a mortal dread in the world it was of this hissing, clanking, smoking monster. If they came upon it by surprise they might find themselves back home or even in the county Clare before they could stop him! They met no monsters, and Father let Barney walk as they came into Nenagh.

They clopped down Kenyon Street and turned into the station yard. They could see the line, and there was no sign of a train. Father went to ask about it, leaving Katie in the trap holding the reins. She looked about with interest at all the activity. A squad of soldiers marched in, halted and were then dismissed. Some lit cigarettes while others looked for shade. An army lorry backed towards her. Perhaps they were expecting supplies on the train. Barney shifted uneasily and Katie wished she was holding his head instead of sitting in the trap, but that would mean dropping the reins while she got out. One of the soldiers in the station doorway hitched his rifle up on his shoulder and walked over. He talked quietly to Barney and stretched up to scratch the horse on the nose. Then his hand slipped down till he was holding the bridle. The lorry backed past.

'Steady, boy,' the soldier said, and looked up at Katie.

'He's quiet,' she said.

'I know that old lorry, it can backfire like a field-gun,' he said, smiling.

Katie looked down into a brown, sunburned face. It was screwed up against the light. She wanted to say something but her wits seemed to have deserted her.

'He's tired as well,' she managed finally.

'Come far?'

'Portroe way.'

'That's over towards the Shannon, isn't it?' He couldn't be much older than Seamus, and not a local either. Galway perhaps, from his accent.

'Yes.' She pulled her thoughts back. 'Up at the slate quarries.' Why couldn't she think of anything better to talk about than old slates?

'Your father in the quarries?' he asked, tipping his head towards the station where Father had disappeared.

'He was till they closed for the war; one of the small quarries.'

'Will they open again?'

'That's what he's trying to do now.'

One of the soldiers over by the station shouted something

and followed it with a guffaw of laughter. The soldier frowned and their conversation faltered. He hitched his rifle up on his shoulder. The sun shone on the oiled wood. Katie found herself staring, fascinated. This was a gun, a real gun, like her father talked about; she'd never been close to one before. It was beautiful but yet terrible at the same time. Was it really made for killing people? It seemed extraordinary that this shiny piece of wood and oiled metal carried death, and for whom?

'Is it heavy?' she asked.

'Oh, you get used to it,' said the soldier, following her eyes. 'We're not supposed to put them down in case they get stolen. It seems there's fighting in Dublin.'

'Who could be fighting now?' Katie asked.

'Soldiers like me fighting soldiers like me.'

'Irish soldiers fighting Irish soldiers? That sounds silly.'

'Yes it is. I thought the treaty Mr Collins brought back was good enough, something to build on; it gave us the Free State, and isn't it freedom we were looking for? But no, the Republicans want nothing less than a Républic – no king. They're ready to fight us for it too.'

'You?'

'Yes, us – the army. So we call them Rebels, and they call us Staters, while the English split their sides laughing. So, there you are,' he said with a grin.

Katie thought of what Mother had said that morning. She didn't know what to say. Was she a Rebel or a Stater? She wanted him to go on talking but a gap was yawning in their conversation. Why had her mouth gone dry? On the butt of the rifle was a triangular patch of lighter wood set into the darker stock.

'What's the yellow triangle for?' she asked, nodding towards it.

'Somebody got a bullet or a bit of shrapnel in it, I reckon,' he said.

'Was he ... hurt?' she said, unhappy at having raised the subject. She had nearly said 'killed'.

'Not by me, at any rate,' the boy laughed. 'I suspect he got the fright of his life though. Maybe it saved him,' he added with a smile, as if to reassure her.

Katie warmed to him. It was nice to have someone reassuring her. She liked him; the day was turning out well. At that moment a bell rang in the station and the signal changed with a clunk.

'That'll be the train,' said the soldier, and Father appeared from the door leading to the platform, walking rapidly.

'Just coming in now,' he said. 'We'd better watch Barney, he might think it's a steam-roller.'

'You go on, Sir, the Miss too, I'll hold him. He'll be all right.'

Father noticed the soldier for the first time. 'Well, thank you very much, young man. Come on, Katie.'

The boy reached up and pulled the horse's head down on to his shoulder and fondled its ears. He smiled at Katie as she passed.

They could see the train approaching down the line as they walked on to the platform. A thin jet of steam shot up once, then twice, and two shrill whistles came down the line.

Everyone stepped back as the engine hissed by. Katie was reminded of the day she had come to fetch her father, but the vapour did not linger as it had on that cold December day. Doors swung open as the train slowed. Her father stood on tiptoe searching over the sudden bustle on the platform. Katie could sense that he was excited.

'There he is – that's Griffith, with the cap – Mr Parry to you – and that must be Dafydd.' He started thrusting his way through the crowd. Katie struggled after him. She could see the man Father had pointed to looking about him, but no sign of his son. A pale gawky lad was helping a lady, his mother perhaps, with a case that looked too heavy for him.

'Griffith!' Father was pumping the man by the hand.

'Sergeant O'Brien, it's good to see you again.'

'Call me Eamonn, or I'll start calling you Captain.'

'There's a threat for you!' and both men laughed, still gripping hands, reluctant to let go.

'Now, where's that son of mine?' asked Mr Parry, looking around.

CHAPTER 3

Dafydd

Katie stood frozen, eyes riveted on the boy who was now grinning amiably up at the two men. It was the sickly lad she had seen. He too wore a cap. His head was small, his ears large; he had a short body with long arms and legs. He seemed to alternate between big and small all the way down, ending in half-mast trousers and a pair of huge hobnailed boots. Katie found herself staring at him in disbelief. Where was the handsome Welsh boy she'd imagined waiting to sweep her off her feet? This boy looked pale and frail with black smudges under his eyes. Only that Father had told her on the way to the station that he was fifteen, she'd have said he was Marty's age, no more. She thought of the picture she had built up of him that morning and felt foolish and resentful all in one. Then she realised they were all looking at her. She tore her eyes away from where they had lodged, on his boots. She could feel a blush rising. It started at her neck and burst on to her face like a flame. The boy seemed to notice. He blinked, as if to adjust to a bright light.

'Pleased to meet you,' he said in a funny sing-song voice, putting out his hand. Then he changed his mind and took off his cap instead. The men laughed. Mr Parry shook her hand and called her beautiful. Father scooped up a sack of tools of theirs, which was lying on the platform, with his hook.

'Your luggage is in the guard's van?' he asked. 'Don't worry about it now, the carter will bring it up this evening as long as it's labelled.' The crowd on the platform was thinning. The soldiers were beginning to file on to the platform. 'We'd better relieve that young man of yours, Katie.'

They found the soldier walking back from the other side of the yard with the trap. Thoughtfully, he had taken Barney away from the line as the train came in.

'You don't like trains, do you, old lad?' the soldier said, patting the horse's neck. 'I'll hold him till you're in, Sir.'

'Katie, you and Dafydd move up to the front, we'll sit in the back and keep the weight off the shafts. Barney will be quiet now, you'll be able to hold him.'

Katie gathered up the reins, feeling a sudden rush of longing. She wanted to stay in Nenagh talking to the handsome soldier with the smiling face and teasing eyes. She knew that he was looking up at her from Barney's head now but she felt too shy to look down. Perhaps he would see what she was feeling. Then she realised she was staring at the boots of the Welsh lad opposite and the two white sticks of his legs emerging from his trousers. She mustn't blush again. She turned to look down at the soldier. He had his head slightly to one side, an eyebrow raised, smiling.

'That's better,' he said quietly, and he might have been saying it to Barney or to her. Then he turned the trap towards the gate and stood back.

'Thank you,' called Father as they passed. 'Hand in that rifle of yours and we'll teach you how to make slates!'

'Soon now,' replied the lad. Then to Katie, 'No reckless driving!'

There were people and carts and a couple of motor cars in the station yard and Katie had to concentrate. But she managed one glance back as she left the yard. He was still there. He raised a hand. Katie wanted to wave back but her hands were full. Then they were in the street being carried along by the flow of traffic.

As they left the town behind them she kept thinking of all the bright, clever things she could have said to the soldier instead of being tongue-tied like a schoolgirl. Then she realised she didn't even know his name! She'd never see him again. How had the beautiful day, which had promised so much, gone wrong? Suddenly she was in a foul temper.

With the two men in the back, the front of the trap was raised like the prow of a ship, and Barney had no weight on him at all. Katie wanted to stand up, like the English queen she had seen in a magazine, driving her chariot to war. Out of the corner of her eye she could see the little Welsh boy. Oh Mother of God! – a summer with those boots! They were clear of the town now. She slapped Barney with the reins, half stood up, collided with the boy's knees and sat down with a jolt. Barney broke into a canter.

'Steady now, Katie,' said her father. She gripped the reins tightly. In the picture, the queen's chariot had had scythes on the wheels. She drove as close as she could to the edge of the road, imagining mowing the dandelions down as if they were her enemies.

By the time the road crossed the Newtown bridge and Barney slowed for the rise through the village, the heat of her anger had passed. She thought she ought to try to be civil. Keeping her eyes away from his boots, she glanced across at the boy. 'Tell me about your quarry. Do you work in it?'

'No, no – still at school I am. Just in the holidays. Odd jobs, like,' again that lilting accent.

The men had stopped talking. 'He splits a very nice slate, does Dafydd,' the boy's father stated.

Dafydd blushed. 'Father's the foreman – see – next to the manager. Met your Dad in the war. Always talking about working with the Irish in the war he is. You see, nobody thought much of the Welsh miners, digging under the German trenches to blow them up. Treated the Welsh like dirt. But the Irish didn't, they were all right. The English didn't like the Irish any more than the Welsh, see. "Two dogs with a bad name," Dad says.'

'But the Irish were fighting *with* England,' said Katie indignantly. 'Dad was a volunteer, "Fighting for the freedom of small nations". Little countries like Belgium!'

'Perhaps it's just because we're both different from the English. Different languages too.'

'Why? What do you speak at home?' asked Katie, surprised.

'Welsh, nothing but Welsh, except in school and with the quarry manager. I like speaking English though.'

'Our teachers are off to school themselves next week to learn Irish. In a few years we'll all be speaking Irish too.'

'I never spoke a word of English before I was six,' said Dafydd. 'That's why Dad wanted me to come. Brush it up, that and ...' He looked up the hill then as something caught his attention and called, 'Hey, Dad, look at the slate tips. Doesn't that make you feel at home?' pointing to the tips of

27

waste slate now just visible from the road.

'Ask him in Welsh,' Katie challenged.

'More than my life's worth.'

They clopped on steadily for a while. Katie was listening to the talk of the men in the back. The news from Dublin sounded serious.

'So you had an exciting time in Dublin?' Katie asked.

'We had no idea there was a war on.'

'I'm sure there isn't really, it's just we all get so excited about politics. Seamus, that's my big brother, and Mother, they are the Republicans in the family. Father is for the Treaty – says we'll never get a better deal out of the English. Nobody wants to fight over it though.'

'Well, they were fighting in Dublin. Never heard such bangs – it was like when we're blasting in the quarry.'

'Oh I'm sure it's nothing. If it is, half the families in Ireland will be split down the middle.' She laughed uneasily, thinking of Mother.

'Hey, Dad,' Dafydd called out. 'Tell them about the station master.'

Mr Parry laughed, shook his head, and said, 'Go on, you tell them.'

Dafydd turned to Katie, who had been watching, with interest, the sun shining pink through his ears. 'We heard the shooting first when the train from Kingstown crossed the bridge over the river ... what was the river, Dad?'

'The Liffey,' said Mr Parry.

'That's it. The railway bridge is high up in the air. We thought the driver stopped because he wanted to see what was happening. Well, I tell you, at the first bang Dad sat up like a hare. You could see his ears twitching.' Dafydd grinned. '"Field gun," Dad says, then there were snapping sounds.

28

"Rifles, several rifles ... listen ... and ... there! a machine-gun," ratta-tat-tat. I was standing at the window, all excited, when a puff of smoke appeared up the river and we heard this big bang. Dad got all heroic then, pulled me back, and sat on me.'

'Don't exaggerate,' laughed Mr Parry, 'you can keep the drama for when you write your journal for Megan – and remember, it *has* to be in English!' Then he turned to Father again. 'Megan's his twin sister,' he explained. 'It did seem though, Eamonn,' he went on, 'that I had jumped out of the fat into the fire. I never thought I'd hear a field-gun fired in anger again.'

'Well, you pinned me back in my seat,' continued Dafydd, undaunted. 'There was a pudgy little man in the carriage too, pressed into the corner, eyes popping, holding his briefcase in front of him for protection. When the train started again we went in a big loop. Past a lot of houses – poor looking – then through a tunnel. I thought that would be the end of it, the shooting I mean, but no, we were shunted backwards into Kingsbridge station which seemed to be right in the thick of it.

'The bangs seemed really close and I wanted to go and have a look, but Dad said that he hadn't survived the war to be shot on his holidays in Dublin. Everyone else was having a peek though, like it was a firework display, not a war. Then along came the station master, very pompous and important he was, like a general conducting a war. He said he was going out to "inspect what was going on". Dad said not to be a fool, but off he marched, straightening his hat. Silence. Then we heard a couple of shots followed by pounding feet, and into the station came the station master, bent double with his hat held over his backside. Talk about indignant! Someone had shot at him!' Katie had to laugh and noticed that Mr Parry joined in.

Katie was not sure what made her turn at that moment. The absence of Father's ready laugh perhaps, or was it that persistent tap-tapping she had been hearing for some time. When she did she gasped. To her horror Father was staring past her, eyes unfocused, a little foam flecking the corner of his mouth, his steel hook going tap-tap, tap-tap on wood of the trap. Memories of Father's madness swept over Katie. She glanced at Mr Parry. He was looking at Father too. Dafydd's voice was prattling on. Barney drifted towards the middle of the road while she was turned. She heard the growl of the approaching lorry too late to do anything about it.

'Look out!' Dafydd yelled as the lorry came around the corner with a snarl and a great gush of black smoke.

Barney side-stepped alarmingly as the lorry nearly grazed the trap. Katie braced her feet, leaning all her weight on the reins to turn his head from the ditch. Out of the corner of her eye, she saw a line of green uniforms and intent faces, the light flashing from the goggles they wore against the dust. Rifles were standing upright between soldiers' knees.

'Crossley Tender,' she shouted to Dafydd as the dust swirled about them. 'See how the soldiers sit back-to-back. Can shoot in any direction.' Barney was still dancing and short-stepping.

'Well done, girl,' Mr Parry said.

Katie's mind went racing back, remembering another day and another road, when the uniforms were not green but were the hateful black and khaki of the Black and Tans – the scum of the British Army and the scrapings of their prisons, Father had called them. It was the last summer of their walks together. There had been room on the road for the English Tender to pass them but the driver had deliberately forced them both into the ditch. The jeering faces of the men looking down were still fixed in her mind, their dust-goggles the glazed eyes of monsters. As they passed they had levelled their rifles at them.

'Get down, Katie,' Father had shouted, pushing her into the ditch and lying on top of her. No shot came; perhaps they were short of ammunition. But she was covered in nettle stings. Later that day, they had climbed together to a place called the Graves of the Leinstermen and sat looking out over the lake. In the scent of summer gorse, while the sun dipped towards the hills of Clare, beyond the Shannon, Father had told her how his regiment had got in the Welsh miners to explode a mine under the Germans and how something had gone wrong – and he had lost his hand. It was then that he had dropped his head and whispered, 'I ran, Katie, God how I ran.'

Which way had he run? Could shame cause madness? Was Father mad? He had never used her name before, not in one of his fits, and to this day she could not tell whether or not he knew that he had told her of these terrible things. She had locked her thoughts up deep inside her and told no-one.

*   *   *

Katie was relieved when home came in sight. Their house always appeared smaller than it really was, set below the level of the road, the farm buildings backed up into the hill, but the walls gleamed white with a dash of blue from the washing-blue her mother ceremoniously added to the barrel of whitewash when it was ready each Easter.

'There we are, that's home,' Katie announced.

'Beautiful,' Dafydd said. 'Hey, Dad, look – it's like snow. Not like our Welsh houses,' adding by way of explanation, 'ours are all dark stone.'

'That's our quarry, straight ahead, past the farm. You can just see the tips and the sheds.' Katie held Barney back firmly as they dipped steeply down through the gate into the farmyard. Marty appeared from an outhouse, saw Katie at the reins, and fled in mock terror.

'That's Marty,' Katie explained resignedly. 'He's the farmer of the family. Don't pay any attention to him, he's always fooling around.' Then she added loudly, so the still-apprehensive head poking round the corner of the shed could hear, 'He's terribly afraid of horses.' Marty came out, grinning sheepishly. As if on cue, Mother appeared from the kitchen and Seamus from the harness room, where he usually went to think; he seldom mended any harness. He was tall, with dark eyebrows that formed a bar across his forehead. He had a slow smile that Katie knew would melt the heart of any girl, if only he would care to use it. He took Barney's head. Katie had loved Seamus with a passion verging on idolatry while Father was away at the war. Later, during the Black and Tan war against the English, while she had looked after Father, Seamus had fretted because he was too young to fight. He'd tell Katie how he'd love to fight for Ireland, but all they'd let him do was run messages.

'Welcome to Tipperary, Dafydd.' Mother was smiling up at the boy. 'Come down now, you must be starved.'

The men climbed down, Katie next, while Marty stood holding the tiny door of the trap as if he were handing gentry out of a coach-and-four. Dafydd followed. He did not see the little iron step at the back of the trap and jumped on to the cobbles with a crash of hobnailed boots. Immediately there was a yip from Marty, who leapt back, holding one foot.

'Dafydd! Did you jump on the lad?' cried Mr Parry in dismay. 'Be careful!'

'Nonsense, he was miles away from him. *Marty!*' yelled Father, 'come here and show some manners. Can you never stop fooling?' Marty, held by the scruff of the neck, but still grinning, was introduced. All at once everyone was talking, and Katie looked at her father laughing and smiling. At least he wasn't going to have a fit now. Marty's clowning had seen to that. It had also cleared her bad temper. She wanted to give Marty a hug, but he didn't look very clean.

*   *   *

'Katie,' said her mother that evening. 'Will you take Marty and Dafydd and show Dafydd where he's to sleep? The boy must be dropping. We have to look after him, you know.'

Humph, thought Katie. She had helped her mother make up the settle bed on the landing while the men walked up to the quarry and Marty showed Dafydd the farm.

'I'd have put Seamus on the landing, but he's too long for the bed,' Mother explained to Dafydd, 'but he and Marty are close beside you in the bedroom, and Katie's room is across the landing, so you won't be lonely.' The settle bed folded away into a chest when not in use, but now it was opened out, the head beside the door leading into the boys' bedroom where the landing was widest. The stairs came up outside Katie's door at the opposite end of the landing. A soap box made a bedside table for a candle, as well as serving for a cupboard for clothes.

Marty was expanding on the probability of Dafydd having to share his bed with a ghost 'the night pusher who ...'

'Will you shut up, Marty,' Katie said. 'The only ghost you'll see about here is Marty creeping around like a blind elephant twice in the night.'

'It's not twice,' he declared indignantly. 'I can't stand using a pot,' he explained, 'the yard's better.'

'You're just not civilised!' said Katie.

'Well, it was you brought the subject up,' he said with some justification. 'I'd like to know ...' he began, but Katie was away down the stairs; she seldom won an argument with Marty and this one was getting out of hand.

It seemed a shame to go to bed when it was so bright. She decided to walk up towards the quarry and meet Father and Mr Parry on their way down.

CHAPTER 4

Up the Republic

Oh Megan, Dafydd wrote to his sister. *I'm in love (again! you say). She's like the rising sun, hair of spun gold. Driving her chariot through this war-torn land. But I, who would be her slave, am in the dog-house. It all started at dinner. Don't ask me how I put my foot in it, but I did, boots and all, and now she's slipped away. They were talking about the fighting in Dublin ...*

* * *

Mother had sniffed the meat anxiously when Katie brought it in from the meat-safe in the dairy, the coolest place on the farm. It had held despite the warm weather. Now the house was filled with the delicious smell of roast lamb, cooked with a sprig of rosemary. This was to be the special welcoming dinner for the two guests, postponed from yesterday when the train was late. Father and Mr Parry had been turned out of the kitchen and were sitting uncomfortably in the parlour with glasses of bottled stout.

'Take care, Katie!' warned her mother, as Katie drew a tray of roast potatoes from the top oven of the range. They spat and pinged in the hot dripping. She loved roast potatoes almost as much as she liked the tiny little new ones which Mother had just shaken out of the pot in a cloud of steam. A knob of yellow butter was turning on them as it melted.

'Where *is* Seamus?' worried her mother. 'I wish he was here.' What was Mother worried about, wondered Katie, Seamus was seldom anywhere when he was wanted; he came and went.

'Look, Katie, would you ever ask Father to sharpen the knife – and don't let Marty near it.'

Seamus had still not appeared when they all sat down and Mother said the few words of Grace. Marty and Dafydd were sitting side-by-side, opposite Katie. She noticed that Dafydd didn't bless himself. Of course, he'd be a Protestant, she remembered, and looked at him with new interest. Then she saw that Marty had noticed too. She could just see some joke or comment working itself out in his mind. Quickly she lashed out at him under the table. To her mortification it was Dafydd who gave a jump.

'Marty,' said Mother severely, 'will you behave yourself there!'

Marty opened his mouth to protest, saw his mother's look, and closed it. Katie kept her eyes down but she could feel both boys' eyes boring into her. A tell-tale blush began to spread from her neck. When she looked up, Dafydd was suppressing a grin, and he and Marty were both ready to explode. She could not trust herself to look again — another moment and they would all three be giggling like children. She mustn't giggle! Not with him. She turned to look up the table, held her breath and forced herself to listen to the adult conversation. Father was stabbing at a piece of meat on his plate.

'Of course you're right, Griff, we should accept the Treaty with the English! It's a step in the right direction, and a step taken without further use of guns. We have Home Rule, let's build on that.'

'What do the Republicans want then?' asked Mr Parry.

'Seamus is the Republican in the family, we should ask him.' Father looked down the table to where Seamus's place stood empty. It was Mother who answered.

'They feel we should throw off the yoke of England completely. Not let the country be divided up into North and South. They think that we stopped just when the war was about to be won. They feel that Mr Collins has betrayed them.'

'That's nonsense, dear. I don't like Mr Collins myself, he's a man of war and I'm sick of men of war, but if I were still a soldier, it is Collins I would follow. Collins knows that he can be beaten. He knows the weaknesses of the English, but he knows our own weaknesses too. That's what separates him from the dreamers. He will do anything, including shooting people in their beds, to make sure he wins.' Father shuddered. 'If he's not fighting now it's because he knows he can't win.'

'But we can win, surely, Eamonn,' said Mother. 'It seemed, only this time last year, that we had the English on the run or holed up in their barracks.' Katie cocked her head. She had never heard Mother speak out like this.

'Arms, my dear, the Irish lack guns and ammunition. One rifle to fifty men, they tell me, that's the first thing. And I say thank God because it means less slaughter, less lives at risk. If we could only get guns out of Ireland ...'

Katie found she'd mashed her new potatoes without thinking and was cross at having spoiled them. Bother him and his guns, she thought. She wanted to hear what Seamus had to say; it wasn't fair to talk like this without him. He's involved in something and I'm being left out of it again, she thought to herself.

'Secondly,' Father went on, 'there is the voice of the people – democracy. We've had elections, you see, Griff. People have voted, and the message is clear. They want the agreement with England, they want the end of the war.'

A shadow darkened the open door.

'*They are traitors!*' The strangled words caught them all by surprise. Chairs scraped on the stone floor as they turned towards the door. Seamus stood there, taut as a bent bow, thin against the light. No-one moved. It was Mother who recovered first.

'Come in, love,' she said, 'we went ahead without you.'

'They are traitors to their oath,' he said without moving. 'They are destroying the most beautiful thing we ever had.'

Katie glanced at her father, but he had managed a smile.

'Come in,' he said, 'tell us, who is destroying what?'

Seamus came forward and took his place stiffly at the end of the table next to Katie. He put his hands on the table and then hurriedly hid them on his lap. She noticed that they were blistered and raw. His plate was passed down and she put it in front of him, but he didn't even look at it.

'The Republic, of course,' he said, glaring up the table.

'But how can they betray something that never existed, Seamus? When did we have a Republic?' protested Father quietly.

'We have it, we have it now – of course it exists!' said Seamus indignantly. 'What about the declaration of 1916? Didn't we declare a Republic then? What about our Dáil, and our army, and our courts? The Republic is ours – we took it from the English.'

'That's the point, son, we haven't taken it from the English. The war isn't over. The trench taken today may be taken back tomorrow. I've seen it. Without a treaty we could lose all we've gained.'

'We'll gain nothing from the English unless we fight for it. The treaty is a betrayal.' Katie sensed that Seamus was very close to tears.

'But the people don't want to go on fighting, Seamie,' Father continued. 'We've had elections. The message from the people is clear; they want the treaty.'

'People!' said Seamus scornfully. 'Where would we be now if we always did what the people wanted? Were the people behind the Fenians? Behind Pearse and Connolly in 1916? Were the people behind us until they saw us beating the Black and Tans? If the people had their way the whole nation would have taken the king's shilling – like *you* – and gone off with Redmond to fight in England's war, and Ireland would have been left to rot!'

A horrified silence filled the room, the insult hanging in the air. Katie was stunned, but at the same time a devil inside her wanted to cheer. Here was her old Seamus, her magnetic, exciting Seamus. She ought to stop him, she knew it, but she had been good for long enough, her whole body was egging him on. She didn't mind if he hurt Father, it was about time Father stopped being frail – and anyway she resented being landed with that plucked chicken of a companion opposite for the summer. She glanced across the table and found herself gazing into the startled eyes of the Welsh boy and she nearly put her tongue out.

Seamus pushed his plate away. 'I heard you; I was outside. But you're wrong – Collins is wrong. We'll find the arms, we'll take the arms from the army and we'll drive the English from Ireland once and for all – from all of Ireland. I'm sick of all this namby-pamby talk. Give me a gun. I'm ready to die for my country. You are all ... all ... *cowards*!' He stood up and his chair fell with a crash as he stumbled towards the door. He turned then, as if to throw one last word at Father, but he faltered. 'Oh God!' he muttered and fled.

*   *   *

Katie listened to his running feet. Then she looked at Father. Sweat beaded his forehead and she could actually see the muscle-chords in his neck as they tightened, pulling at his lower jaw. To her horror she realised she was seeing all the symptoms of one of his madness attacks. But this was in front of the whole family, in front of strangers! His madness was back and God knows what was going to pour out. If she could just reach his hand she'd squeeze the life out of it. When he did begin to speak his voice was high and unnatural.

'My boy wants a gun. Do you remember the machine-guns that night, Griff, the night we blew the mine? They had a menace I'd never heard before. They were ... what is the word, Griff? So ... so ...' The pauses got longer. 'So ... '

Katie held her breath. Quiet, everybody, quiet, she willed, please, not a word and it may pass. She heard the blood hissing in her ears. A word, a cough even, and it would all come spilling out. Did anyone else know he had run away? 'God how I ran!' he had said. Please, Mary Mother of God, let no one speak, she prayed. I've kept his secret, don't let him give himself away now.

'The guns were so ...'

Then it came, one word, sing-song, rising and falling, completely Welsh.

'Angry?' said Dafydd.

Katie stared at the boy across the table, wishing him dead and waiting for Father's crazed reaction. She wanted to cover her head. But the atmosphere in the room was changing. There were small movements – a knife was scraped on a plate, a cup rattled, someone coughed. She raised her head. The chords on her father's neck were disappearing; he was smiling to himself, massaging his neck. Had the attack passed?

'Thank you, Dafydd. That is the word, *angry*. You never

forget the anger of war, do you, Griff?' He turned to Mr Parry. 'I still find myself back there at times, you know.'

'We all do,' said Mr Parry. 'Touch of shell-shock. Not surprising is it?'

Katie sat rigid. What had happened? Everyone was talking normally. It wasn't fair. She stared at Father but he was reaching for another potato. He looked pleased with himself. Now her anxiety was turning to anger. All those years of torture, of listening, keeping his secrets, and now, because there were visitors, he could suddenly pull himself together, just like that, and help himself to another potato!

He straightened up. 'Now, what am I to do about my son? Griff, you and I must make a future for him. He could do more for Ireland by learning to split slates than by finding a gun.'

No one seemed to notice when Katie left the room and climbed the stairs. She closed the door of her bedroom and lay face down on her bed. For a long time she was too angry to cry. She lay dry-eyed while resentment throbbed inside her like a lump of hot lead. Tears, when they came, hurt too much to bring relief.

CHAPTER 5

Frog!

'Go away,' said Katie, lifting her face from her sodden pillow. She knew it was Father who had tapped on the door and she hated him. She pulled the pillow up about her ears so she wouldn't hear if he knocked again. She hated him with all her heart. All those wasted years when she could have been having fun with friends of her own. Hadn't *she* nursed him back from the dead? Hadn't *she* listened while he sicked up all the filth of his beastly war? And she had thought he was mad, or ashamed! Oh no! touch of shell-shock, Mr Parry had called it. What was shell-shock anyway? And what right had Father to criticise Seamus? Seamus wasn't running away as he had.

Father's steps receded down the stairs and a fresh bout of tears and resentment shook her. She thought of all those times when she had listened, biting her tongue, hardly daring to breathe, when an attack came on him. She had loved him then and they had fought his battles together, she herding him back from the edge of madness like a small sheepdog. But he'd forgotten her now. All that was over. All it took to cure him now was one word from a pallid Welsh boy. 'Thank you, Dafydd,' he'd said, nice as pie. Who cared about Katie now? He might as well have slammed the door in her face.

She came up for air, her face burning with resentment. What right had that boy to come and upset it all? It was his fault. She thought with disgust of his boots and the sun shining through his prominent ears, and his sing-song voice. 'Angry' was all he had said. Katie repeated it to herself, with heavy sarcasm. Perhaps if she had looked like a frog in boots and had croaked 'Angry' in a soft Welsh voice, she could have cured Father of his fits without having had to listen to his beastly tales. She'd be the one he loved now. Katie knew she was being unjust – but it was about time she was unjust to someone. She was pleased with the idea of Dafydd as a frog; one can hate a frog without committing a mortal sin. She imagined a whole line of frogs all croaking: Angry ... angry ... angry, at different pitches but all with Welsh accents. Suddenly they started to sing in harmony.

*　　*　　*

She woke when her father tapped on the door for a second time. Her tears had dried, leaving her face feeling stiff. He came in.

'Did you drop off?' He sat down on the edge of her bed and smoothed the hair out of her eyes. She pulled back. 'You've been crying.'

'I'm all right now.'

'Did I give you a fright at dinner? Quite like old times – and I thought I was over all that. Perhaps Mr Parry is right, perhaps I was shell-shocked.'

'What is shell-shock?' asked Katie dully.

'I suppose you could call it being scared out of your wits. It affects your mind – you can't face up to the memories perhaps? To things you have seen, or done.'

'Oh.'

'I'll be all right though. I've got Mr Parry here now. He'll help. He's been through it all too, you see. I've not had anyone here to share it with, not the bad bits that is.'

A huge silent scream rose in Katie: *What about me?*

But he was talking again. 'Funny about Dafydd, over here

to brush up on his English, and he's the one to find a word for me.'

Katie closed her eyes and clamped her mouth shut.

'Is there something wrong, Katie?' he asked. 'Have I said something?' She shook her head and stared bitterly in front of her. All she had wanted since that winter day on the platform at Nenagh was to be his, to find his love and to fan it, from glow, to spark, to fire, but now that he found he could be cured with a word from a total stranger, he was stamping on her, coldly and deliberately. 'I'll be all right,' he went on. 'I don't need you so much now. You should get out more and be with your friends, be free.'

Katie couldn't believe what she was hearing. She closed her eyes and tried to listen to sounds outside the room, but there were none. Then she became aware of his voice again.

'... perhaps *you* could talk to him.'

'Who?' she asked.

'Seamus.'

She stared past his shoulder out of the window. Seamus ... something stirred her interest. Life was straightforward for Seamus; he had a cause. So, Father wanted her to talk to him, did he? She was tempted to say something bitter, but interest was pricking her again. Instead she said, 'Why not Mother – or Marty?'

'Marty's too young, and Mother ... Mother thinks that if she were to go for him he'd be shamed and wouldn't come home.'

'Where is he?'

'She thinks he's up at Uncle Mal's.'

'They're Republicans, aren't they?'

'Yes, they're not fat farmers like us. The mountainy people were strong in the fight against the English. They see the treaty as a defeat.'

43

'Mother does too. She's a mountainy person; that used to be her home up there,' said Katie. 'I like Uncle Mal. He laughs a lot.'

'So do I, and I'm sure he'd keep Seamus out of trouble if he could, but there are people about who would regard Seamus as just so much cannon-fodder.'

Katie thought, but Seamus *wants* to be cannon-fodder, then, spitefully, and *he* wouldn't run away. 'Is there going to be fighting, then?' she said aloud.

'It's looking like civil war, love. Irish fighting Irish; why oh why can't we give up guns and use our brains instead!'

Katie swung her legs to the floor. She was suddenly sick of using her brains. If Irish were going to fight Irish you had to be on one side or the other. If Father didn't need her now, perhaps Seamus did. She remembered how, years ago, before Father came home, she had been Seamus's self-appointed slave. He had burned with ideals even then and found a small sister a useful acolyte. She in turn had worshipped him, a faithful follower fuelling his imagination.

Father reached over to stroke her hair, but she pulled away, knelt on the window ledge and looked down into the yard. It seemed empty. Hens were fluffed out in dust bowls in the shade of the cart shed. She could see Dafydd sitting on the shaft of the big farm cart writing, a letter in English perhaps. As she watched he scratched the top of his head with his pencil, grinned and wrote laboriously on. Katie drew back into the room. She didn't want him to see her. Father was standing watching her. She made for the wash-stand and he stepped back out of her way.

'I'll go,' she said. 'I'll go now,' splashing water over her face. 'But Seamus won't come home.'

'I know he may not, but you'll try, won't you? Tell him he's welcome back; his home is here, whatever his cause. Who's to say who's right and who's wrong in politics? But let him leave the guns behind. Guns have no rightful place in the future of Ireland.'

Katie dried her face, burying it in the towel. If only he wasn't so reasonable! It was irritating. To her surprise she had a quick, uninvited vision of a brown, smiling face looking up from Barney's head, a rifle slung casually over one shoulder. It was a ray of former happiness. She pushed it out of her mind. If Ireland needed Seamus, perhaps it needed her as well ... but Father was talking again; why couldn't he be quiet?

'You can take Dafydd with you for company. He's outside in the yard, writing a letter.'

'No!' she shouted, stamping and throwing her towel on the floor. 'Why should I? Why him! If I go at all I'll go on my own!'

'Whisht, dear, whisht. The lad's just outside. I thought you liked him? He'll be company.'

'I hate him! I hate his boots.'

'His boots!' laughed Father. 'The poor lad's been sick. He's convalescing. We've got to look after him.'

'Is that why he looks like a sick chicken? What's the matter with him?'

'Now, Katie! He's had scarlet fever and very nearly died, I hear.'

'The walk would be too much for him then,' she said.

'He's convalescent, Katie, not sick. He needs three things – food, sun and exercise – and that's the least we can give when Mr Parry has come all this way just to help me. Anyway, you must have someone with you. These are troubled times, Katie. I don't want you on the roads alone.'

Why had she mentioned those damned boots? What was the point? Well, perhaps she could turn Dafydd into a rebel too. She slipped her shoes on and ran down the stairs.

*   *   *

'Come, Frog, we're going for a walk.'

Dafydd looked up in surprise, then realised she was speaking to him. He closed the exercise book he had been writing in and clattered off to put it back into the house. She listened while he thumped up the stairs. There were sounds of a mild collision, Father coming down probably, then the clatter of descending boots. She turned up towards the gate. Convalescent or not, let him run.

She turned left, back the way they had driven in, to where the road from the house met the steeper winding road up to the mountain. Katie kept up a brisk pace but the scrunch of Dafydd's boots drew steadily closer. She pulled off her shoes and slid them upside-down into the hedge. She would be faster barefoot. The warm dust of the road felt good after her shoes, which were getting too tight for her anyway. The road was too steep to run, and fresh stone chippings had been scattered in places, so she jumped from smooth patch to smooth patch. Dafydd's boots reproached her from behind; they must weigh a ton. She stopped and waited until he came into view round the bend below.

'Saint's above, Frog,' she called, 'will you take those boots off and walk like a Christian!' Dafydd stopped, looked at his boots, and looked up the hill at her. 'Shove them in the wall, we'll pick them up when we come back.' Undoing the laces seemed to take ages, as he crouched in the road with his knees by his ears. 'Frog,' Katie repeated to herself with satisfaction. Off came the socks. She watched while he took his first steps – it was like someone stepping on to thin ice. 'Mother of God,' she muttered, 'he can't even walk barefoot. Well,' she determined, turning back to the hill, 'he'll have to learn.'

*   *   *

Mick-the-Shilling was sitting in the sun beside the road at the top of the hill. There was no avoiding him, but he was harmless and Katie wanted a rest. Most of her anger had dissolved by now and she wanted to think about what she would say to Seamus, so she sat down on the opposite side of the road. Mick could not talk, but rolled his head and grunted.

'Aaaah waaa,' he said.

'Hello, Mick,' she said. 'Fine day.'

'Aaah aaah,' he replied, nodding vigorously. His head swung about aimlessly, then stopped; he was looking downhill. Katie didn't want to see Dafydd's progress below so she lay back and watched the little puffy clouds through the branches of an old pine tree above. After a bit the clouds seemed to stand still, and the tree and the whole world were turning under her and she gripped the grass with her hands so she wouldn't fall off the earth. Then she realised that Mick-the-Shilling was whimpering. She tried to ignore him, but the whimpering continued, puppy-like, and she had to look. He was waiting to catch her eye, his mouth grinning and drooling, but his eyes looked troubled. With his hands he began imitating a puppy's wobbly walk. He whimpered and blew on his paws and licked them as if they hurt, then glanced down the road. Katie would have laughed but she knew what he was saying and felt guilty. Nevertheless, she was damned if she was going to let a half-wit tell her what to do. She got up and turned to go on. To her embarrassment, Mick growled. Not a puppy growl, but a menacing-dog growl. She was frightened and a little bit shamed. She turned and looked down the hill. Poor Dafydd was making very heavy weather of it. He looked just like Mick-the-Shilling's puppy. Katie laughed, but she felt sorry for the boy.

'Walk on the smooth bits,' she called, 'where the cart wheels have gone, or on the grass.'

Dafydd looked up gratefully and waved. If he could have blown on his feet, he would. Eventually he flopped down on the grass beside Katie with a sigh. 'We ... live in the village, see. Not allowed in the quarries without proper boots ... crush your toes.'

'Dafydd, this is Mick-the Shilling. He doesn't speak.' Katie turned to Mick. 'Dafydd is from Wales. His Dad's in the slate quarries there. They've come over to help us get our pit going.'

Mick nodded and grinned. He began to mime picking up an imaginary block of slate and setting it carefully between his feet.

'Watch him,' Katie said. Mick took up an invisible hammer and chisel, as if he had had them lying ready beside him. Working around the block, Mick split off an imaginary slate and offered it to Dafydd, who half got up to take it before remembering it wasn't there.

'Fooled you there, Frog,' said Katie, not unkindly, 'but we should get on to Uncle Mal's.' She got up and turned to go.

'Nnnyaa nnn!' Mick was flapping his hands urgently.

'What's the matter, Mick?'

He abandoned his noises. He was furtive now – hiding something? What was that in his hands? A gun! Sure as day.

'Man – men with guns? Right, Mick? Up at Uncle Mal's?' Mick was nodding vigorously now. 'Will we go the front way?' Mick shook his head. 'The back way then?' Mick nodded but put a finger to his lips.

'Come on then, Frog, it's over the fields for us. It seems the whole Republican army is protecting our brave Seamus – it'll be kinder on your feet too. Thank you, Mick.' Katie climbed the wall where slabs of slate had been inserted to make steps and dropped down into the field. While Dafydd climbed she looked back. Mick-the-Shilling was staring after Dafydd and making frog-hops in the road. Katie smiled.

'Come on, Frog,' she called, and set off across the field.

CHAPTER 6

Civil War

Katie had always loved Uncle Mal's Farm. It nestled within a group of gnarled pine trees at the head of a wide valley. Above the house the mountain rose in curves of soft heather so springy you could roll down the slope without hurting yourself, sneezing in a cloud of pollen. She used to think the valley had been made by some giant when the mountain was still soft, pressing his thumb into its side. He was a giant with green fingers though, because where he had pressed hardest the valley was green with grass. The path they were following was a mere groove in the meadow, but she knew it well. It led through a neighbour's farm and thence by a lane to her uncle's back door. Grasshoppers pinged off their legs as they walked.

'That's Uncle Mal's, over there in the trees, but we have to go through the neighbour's first,' she said.

'Isn't that trespassing?' asked Dafydd anxiously.

'What? They won't mind – isn't it all Ireland!' But she added, 'It would be good if their dog didn't bark though.' There was nobody about. They tiptoed past the front of the house. The dog was there; he lifted his head off his paws, looked at them, and lowered it with a sigh. They entered the lane. Katie was nervous; she could have done without having to bring the boy with her.

'Look,' she said, 'this could be dangerous. You don't have to come.'

Dafydd's eyes widened. 'I'll come,' he said.

'Right then,' she commanded. 'You stay three steps behind me, keep down and when I stop, you stop.' The lane was little used, and overhung with scarlet fuchsia flowers. She wondered what to expect. Mick-the-Shilling probably didn't know what he was talking about, you wouldn't know what might be going on in his mind. She glanced back. Dafydd was copying her every move.

The little iron gate from the lane into the yard stood open. Foot by foot she crept forward, on all fours now, dress clutched in her fist, watching where she put her hands and knees. She turned in at the gate, looked up cautiously, then froze. She was staring at the patched seat of a man's trousers. He was standing not three feet in front of her and he had a gun under one arm. She turned to Dafydd and put a finger to her lips. If only she'd come along the lane whistling. God only knew what the man might do if he turned now. Her mouth felt dry. She was so close she could touch him. She began to back away, hand and then foot, when all at once a stone began to turn under her knee. There was only one thing to do – say something.

'Aa-hem,' she said.

To her amazement the man literally leapt in his standing. 'Jesus-Mary-and-Joseph!' he said, spinning round. His gun fell to the ground with a clatter.

'Josie!' she said, recognising him. It was Uncle Mal's farmhand. 'It's me – Katie. Don't shoot.'

'How can I bloody well shoot with my gun on the ground? What are you doing anyway, Katie O'Brien, frightening an honest rebel out of his wits?'

'Is Seamus in there, Josie? I *must* see him.'

'Where else?' He picked up his gun and wiped the dust off it. Katie turned to where Dafydd stood in the lane, still frozen like someone playing Grandmother's Footsteps.

'Come on, Dafydd,' she said beckoning with her head. 'It's all clear.'

Josie jumped. 'Holy Mother of God, another one! I'm surrounded.'

'Dafydd's from Wales. He doesn't speak a word of English,' lied Katie with sudden inspiration, glaring at Dafydd. 'He's come to learn.'

'Well, he'll get enough chat out of you, anyway,' Josie stated. Katie put her tongue out. 'You'll find them all in the parlour,' he went on. 'There's an officer up from Cork in there, a big nob.'

'Thank you, Josie, you'll take care of that gun now, won't you?'

'You won't go telling on me, child, will you? It's only an old shotgun.'

'Child?' said Katie scornfully.

Josie turned to Dafydd. 'You have a hard woman there, Dafydd, haven't you, lad?' Dafydd looked at him blankly. Josie groaned and scrubbed at his forehead. 'It's not my day, is it? Get along with you, the pair of you.'

*   *   *

As they crossed the yard Katie wondered what had possessed her to say that Dafydd knew no English. He was bound to give himself away. But she needed space, space to tackle Seamus on his own. They could hear a precise, commanding voice declaiming inside. The kitchen door was open. Katie turned to Dafydd.

'Remember, you don't know English, not a word of it. If they talk to you, answer in Welsh.'

'Gorwedd Draig Cymru wrth dy draed.'

'What?'

'*Draig Cymru; ond chwarae â thân yr wyt ti.*'

'Not me, you mutt!' she said, glaring at him. 'Now, shut up.' Dafydd looked disappointed. 'All right, clever Frog, fooled Katie. Now, come on.' She hesitated when she got to the doorway. She wasn't going to try creeping up on anyone again. At first sight the kitchen was empty. To her left the parlour door stood open. She could see the backs of men sitting; others were standing along the walls. A board was balanced on the mantelpiece with a map sprinkled with different-coloured dots. She couldn't see the speaker until he stepped forward to jab at a point on the map. She got a glimpse of a trench coat then and wondered that anyone could wear a coat in that heat. Her uncle Mal sat under the map, looking pink and uncomfortable, with an arm-band on his arm.

As Katie's shadow fell across the kitchen floor heads turned in the dark of the kitchen and she realised that there were people in there too, clustered about the door. Someone said, 'Shssssh!' as Auntie Nora came tip-toeing across.

'Come in, Katie darling,' she whispered. 'But be quiet as a mouse. And who's your friend?' putting a welcoming hand on Dafydd's shoulder.

'Dafydd's from Wales – he doesn't speak a word of English.' Katie hoped the low light in the kitchen would hide her blush.

'He's welcome, but we mustn't disturb the meeting. We have an officer up from Cork.' She winked at Dafydd, put her finger to her lips and guided him to the chair that she had been sitting on at the parlour door. The disturbance was noticed inside.

'Who's there? Who's out there?' demanded the voice.

'Just family,' called Auntie Nora, 'just the childer.'

Katie waited till the voice started again. 'Where's Seamus, Auntie Nora? Is he here?'

'Indeed he is. Is it urgent? I don't like to interrupt.'

'It is urgent,' Katie said, nodding. If she waited till the meeting broke up she'd never get Seamus alone. Also, she was beginning to regret having told lies about Dafydd; he was bound to give himself away. Her aunt leaned into the room, tapped someone on the shoulder and pointed. Katie grimaced as chairs moved and feet shuffled. At that moment Seamus appeared in the doorway. Behind him the voice said sharply: 'Can I please have some order here. This is a briefing not a parish meeting. I'll now call on ... '

Katie had a smile ready for Seamus when he came out, but when he saw who it was, he nearly turned back. White with anger, he pushed her backwards across the kitchen and out the door.

'What are you doing here?' he whispered angrily. 'Look what you've done! Do you realise who that is in there! You have me shamed.'

'I want to help, Seamus. I want to do something for Ireland, like you. I'm fed up with sitting at home.'

'Mother of God! Is that all you've come to say?'

'I have a message from Father too,' she stammered.

'What's his message?'

'He ... he sent me ... but I wanted to come anyway. He says come back, that he respects –'

'Respects!' spat Seamus. 'Come away from the door. What side are you on? How did you get in here without being stopped?'

Katie thought of nice Josie and his shotgun and kept her mouth shut. Seamus was pushing her across the yard. The door of the barn was open and he pulled her in behind it. There was a low growl from the dark behind them, perhaps Uncle Mal's bitch had pups? Katie's carefully rehearsed speech deserted her.

'Seamus – your dream – of Ireland as it should be. I heard what you said at dinner today. Mother thinks like that too, doesn't she? What should *I* think? I want to do something for Ireland too, you know. Father doesn't want me any more and I'm ready to help. I want to do something.'

'What can *you* do?' Seamus's scorn cut into her.

'We used to plan, and do things together. Surely ...'

'We were children then. Grow up! There won't be a future unless we fight for it – and girls are no good at fighting.'

'That's stupid! But why must we fight? Isn't there some other way? Father says ...' She hadn't meant to mention Father again.

'Don't talk about him!' Seamus shouted and then dropped his voice. 'I'm fed up with Father. He's gun-shy, he's like ... he's like a spoiled spaniel ... worse than no dog at all. He's not a man any more, Katie. I saw him at dinner. Keep him out of it. If we're to win this battle we can't have passengers; nurse him, and keep him out of my way. We need men who know how to use a gun.'

Katie backed up against the barn door. There was a bitterness in Seamus's voice, something cold and resentful, which confused her. She had come with an open mind to offer herself to his cause, but this Seamus frightened her. She snapped back, 'You don't have a gun, do you? You're just a dog without teeth.'

'But I'll get one.'

'How?'

'Find that out for yourself.'

'I will. And what happened to your hands? They're all blistered, I saw them at dinner.'

'All right, I haven't got a gun now but there are other ways of fighting the enemy,' said Seamus. 'Cutting off his communications, for one. That's what the officer is explaining inside,

54

but we've been at it already, cutting trees down so that they fall across the roads. The plan is to bring the whole country to a halt using fallen trees, digging trenches in roads, lifting railway lines and blowing up bridges.'

'But these are *our* bridges and *our* railways, how does that change things? That won't win a war!' said Katie.

'Oh yes it will. It means we can cut the Free Staters off in their barracks, just as we did the English. If they can't get reinforcements we can pick them off and capture their weapons.'

'Like where? What barracks would you attack?'

'Well, a town not far from here –'

'Nenagh! But ...' Katie's voice faded.

'What?'

'But there are hundreds of soldiers there, I've seen them.'

'So?' Seamus glanced around. 'Those troops are not all for the Free State, you know, there are good Republicans there too.' He dropped his voice. 'In the next few days half that garrison will come out for us.'

'You mean change sides without fighting?'

'Oh no, there'll be fighting all right. It's not just the men we need, but the guns and ammunition the Free State troops are holding as well. There'll be bloodshed, no getting away from it,' he said with relish.

Katie felt as if her chest were in a clamp. She was beginning to see for the first time that what was happening was real. She remembered a smiling face looking up at her from Barney's head. I'm for the Free State, the boy had said. Katie stammered, 'But the men who change sides, they'll be traitors won't they, betraying their friends?'

'Jesus, child, grow up – don't you understand anything? It is the government troops that are the traitors. They have betrayed the Republic and the Dáil for their half-breed Free State. Do you realise they're asking us to take an oath of allegiance to the King of England. Never! Who are the traitors now?'

'But it means killing our ... our friends, Seamie. Killing people who fought with us against the English. Friends like ... like ...' she had to stop.

'You can't make an omelette without breaking eggs. You have to be trained. You have to stop thinking of the enemy as a person. When you see a man in green uniform in the sights of your rifle, and begin to squeeze the trigger, it is not an Irishman or a friend who is about to die, but a traitor. That Irishman died when he swore away his birthright.' Seamus spoke as if reciting something he'd learned by heart. He was pacing, obviously wanting to get back to the meeting. 'Squeeze the trigger,' he said under his breath as if repeating a lesson. Then he turned towards her. 'Go back and nurse Father, Katie. I'll come home from time to time if I'm let. But I'm not going to stop doing what I think is right, for you or anyone. You've got to realise we have to get the British out now – right out for ever!' To her amazement then he put his arms around her.

For a second Katie didn't know what to do. It was an invitation for her to come back: big brother, little sister. But that was gone, done with, finished. I'm for the Free State, the boy at Nenagh had said. Seamus had no right to kill him just because of that. With an energy that surprised her, Katie pushed Seamus away.

'Come back or not as you like,' she snapped. 'Just keep the war away from home. I'll fight this my own way. Keep away from Father too. I could do without you upsetting him as you did today.'

There was a rustle in the straw in the barn. Katie's eyes were adjusted to the dark now and she could make out two eyes and the outline of a dog, head raised, teeth showing. There was another growl.

'Shut up!' she said to it, and turned away, striding towards the house to collect Dafydd.

'What do you mean, fight this your own way?' asked Seamus, hurrying after her.

'Work that out for yourself, soldier,' she retorted.

It was only when she and Dafydd were out in the lane that she thought about the dog again; it had been black, black without a patch of white. Uncle Mal had no dog like that! It made her spine tingle but she was glad she had told it to shut up. To hell with the black dogs.

*   *   *

Dafydd sat beside the road and laced up his boots.

'Oh, the comfort of a pair of socks,' he said with a sigh.

They had hardly spoken on the walk back. Katie had been preoccupied.

'How much did you hear – of what the man was saying up at the house? What they're planning?'

'Me? Never understood a word. I'm Welsh, you see,' said Dafydd.

Katie looked at him with interest.

CHAPTER 7

Informer!

'Squeeze the trigger,' the voice said, but Katie's arms were aching and she couldn't hold the heavy rifle steady. The sights weaved and bobbed. Sometimes she had the advancing soldier dead-centre in the frame, then, just as her finger curled on the trigger he would bob away. She knew who the soldier was because it was *his* rifle she was holding – the triangle of yellow wood where it had been repaired was silky smooth against her cheek.

'Squeeze the trigger!' It was a command. The soldier was closer now and unarmed. Did that make a difference? 'Now!' All she could see was the green of his uniform filling the whole of her vision. She could not miss! She would look up when she fired; she had to see his face, the face of a man without a birthright.

The kick of the rifle and the crash of the shot came as one. As the soldier's knees bucked under him, Katie looked up into the dying face – looked and disbelieved. It wasn't him. There was something terribly wrong – the hair a fuzz of red, the eyes that were glazing over were blue. It was her own face.

'Poor country – poor poor country, no – no – poor Katie,' she grieved.

*　　　*　　　*

She stared up into the dark of her room, her pulse racing. What had woken her? The stairs creaked – Seamus? No, Marty surely, on his nightly expedition. Probably tripped over the Frog's boots, that would have been the crash. But the confusion of her dream seemed to have cleared her mind. She had felt lost, bereaved almost, when they had got back from Uncle Mal's. Now she began to plan, quickly and clearly. When she was satisfied that her plan would work, she slept.

*   *   *

Katie woke, pleased to find her plan still neat and clean in her head. She met Marty at the top of the stairs.

'Look who's after early worms,' he said.

'Shhh.' Katie put her finger to her lips and pointed to the settle where Dafydd slept, humped in the bed. Marty winked and tiptoed pointedly down the stairs and into the kitchen.

She wasn't often up this early, and she felt nervous. But the homely smell of the kitchen calmed her. The range, which was kept in with a couple of sods of turf, scented the room. The pendulum clock on the wall ticked hollowly. Prince stirred from his place beside the range, got up, stretched stiffly and walked, tail wagging, towards the kitchen door. Marty let him out and followed him into the yard. The light outside was still colourless, the sun not yet up. Katie put on an apron and opened the door of the range. She riddled the ashes off the turf carefully and dropped a handful of kindling through the hole in the top plate. Then she blew, closing her eyes against the waft of dust which swirled back out at her. She persisted until the twigs crackled into life, then added a shovelful of coal from the hod. The porridge had been left soaking on the back of the range overnight. She moved it on to the hot-plate and began to stir.

Marty came in with a jug of buttermilk and a slab of butter from the dairy.

'Don't you drink all of that,' she said. 'I want to make a loaf. Dafydd has all the bread eaten.'

'Well, well, well – what's all this sudden virtue?' Marty looked at her with his head to one side. 'Could someone have committed a little sin, perhaps, a little crime, or could there be one in the planning?' He cut a slice from the heel of the loaf and spread it thickly with butter. Katie turned her back on him and stirred the porridge.

'Don't go losing your bread under all that butter,' she said.

'Oh ho!' said Marty through his mouthful, 'if it was a past sin we wouldn't be all bossy, so it's a sin in the making, is it? That's interesting now!' Katie set her mouth. Marty had a disconcerting way of seeing through her. As he munched, Marty hummed knowingly.

'Look!' she said in exasperation. 'Will you get out of here, look after your blessed cows and mind your own business.'

Marty edged towards the door. 'It had better be a good one. The last sin ... ouch!' he was gone.

Katie walked over and picked up the porridge spoon and wiped the mess off the door with her apron. She could hear him already calling 'Hup hup,' for the cows down the lane. 'Bother!' she muttered under her breath. The plan that had seemed so clear as she lay in bed now seemed wild and improbable. 'Damn Marty!' She pushed the porridge off the hot-plate to the back of the range and closed the lid so the heat would build up in the oven while she mixed the bread. She would not be put off.

*   *   *

'Now, that's a smell to gladden you,' said Father, sniffing as he came into the kitchen.

'Isn't she great,' said Mother. 'She has half my day's work done for me.' Mr Parry came in from the yard, his hair glistening with water. Katie heated the pot for tea. There was a thunder of boots on the stairs and Dafydd appeared. His hair was tousled and he carried the pot from under his bed in front of him. He checked, saw everybody, then made an embarrassed dash for the door. Everyone looked somewhere else.

'Well, what do you want us to do today, Eamonn?' asked Mr Parry, pouring cream on to his porridge.

'We won't get the men up today, not Saturday. The ones I want will be busy – and you can keep the others,' said Father. 'Let you and me take a really good look at the place today. We'll be ready then for the men tomorrow. Father MacDonagh has promised to make an announcement for me at Mass. We'll have more men and advice than we want before Sunday's out.' Dafydd looked up at his father and raised a questioning eyebrow.

'Sunday already?' Mr Parry sounded surprised.

'Why yes. Oh! I forgot, of course you don't work or even discuss work on a Sunday, do you? How foolish of me.'

'Time was it was strictly the Lord's Day but the war changed all that. Anyway, this is Ireland, not Wales.'

'We must see that you get to church, though. There's the Church of Ireland –'

'Don't you worry, we're chapel people, you see, but ever since the war I've learned to find God in silence. Do you remember how the nightingales sometimes sang before the guns started in the war? Your hills will do Dafydd and me just fine. If it is too quiet I will get him to sing, and that's a threat. I haven't managed to get a cheep out of him since his voice broke.'

'I wonder if there's any news of the trouble in Dublin,' Father mused. 'We could do with a newspaper.' Katie, whose thoughts had been elsewhere, looked up sharply.

Mr Parry added, 'Dafydd could do with news too, couldn't you, lad? He's all keen to hear how the mountaineers are doing on Mount Everest. Met them, he did, up at Llyn Ogwen, practising.'

'There was Mr Mallory and Mr Irvine,' said Dafydd. 'They had ropes and boots with special nails along the edges.' Katie hadn't expected Dafydd to have an interest in climbing. He had caught the sun on their walk and looked less cadaverous now. Also, he had a phenomenal appetite.

'I think that's where Dafydd's liking for boots comes from,' laughed Mr Parry, but Dafydd went on, 'There was an Irish man there too – a Mr O'Brien, just like you. He climbed barefoot. You couldn't climb on Everest barefoot though, you'd get frost-bite. Perhaps they've got to the top by now. It takes weeks and weeks for news to come back.'

'Dafydd and me'll go and get a *Nenagh Guardian*, or an *Independent*,' said Katie.

Dafydd looked surprised, then looked across at his father, questioning. The men got up.

'That's kind,' said Mr Parry. 'You can come up to the quarry when you get back, Dafydd.' As their voices receded across the yard Katie heard Mr Parry ask, 'Is it far?'

'No, you can walk across the fields.' Katie coughed to drown Father's words. Marty thumped her heartily on the back, saying, 'That's for your sins.'

*   *   *

'Start at the edge, dip the skimmer in steeply, then flatten it out just under the cream.' Dafydd did as he was instructed. 'Now pull it towards you.' The thick layer of yellow cream crumpled up on to the enamel skimmer while the blue milk flowed out through the holes. 'Keep it flat and lift it over the bowl – keep it flat! There, easy isn't it?' Katie stepped back and glanced cautiously out the dairy door. She was just in time to see her mother, looking smart, set off up the yard. She would be going to see Mrs Moran about the summer sale. Marty had gone down to the wet meadows to look at the bullocks. She could hear the swish-swish of Peter sweeping out the byre; she could manage Peter. Dafydd had not done badly. There were still islands of cream floating on the milk. She swept these up expertly. Mother still made butter for their own use. Katie promised herself she would help her with the churning this evening. She covered the bowl and the cream with muslin.

*   *   *

'Are you sure it's all right, your taking the trap?' asked Peter as he fitted Barney into his harness.

'Yes, we have a message,' said Katie, trying not to be caught in a lie.

'Take care then, he's fresh,' said Peter, stepping back.

Katie looped the reins over her hands, hoping she didn't look as scared as she felt.

'I thought your Dad said it was a walk through the fields?' said Dafydd.

'It's quicker by trap,' she said, 'quicker where we're going.'

She was only just in control as they rattled down the pot-holed road from the farm and they approached the main road at a trot. At the junction the road rose steeply up left into the village. Dafydd adjusted his grip, bracing himself for the turn, but next moment he was on his back on the floor of the trap. Without slackening pace, Katie had turned right, away from the village on to the road to Nenagh.

'Gid-up, Barney,' she called as Dafydd floundered about at her feet. The crash of his fall had frightened Barney, who trotted faster, ears back, a short jerking motion. Katie stood up and braced her feet apart. She hadn't changed her clothes before coming out. Her blouse was old, her skirt patched – and she wanted to sing. She pulled the ribbon from her head and shook her hair free. Dafydd had clambered on to the seat and was holding on grimly; his ears flashed as they passed in and out of sunlight, but Katie was thinking of someone else. *He* would know what to do, when she found him, and between them they would stop this fight, perhaps even the whole war.

She imagined their meeting clearly. In the street, or perhaps down at the railway station again. He'd be there, smiling a surprised greeting. She'd drag Barney to a halt. Then, leaning from the trap, she'd tell him that a mutiny was planned. She imagined him looking up at her, as he had at the station, eyes intent but smiling. Perhaps he'd put his hand in hers for a second, but there'd be no time for more. He'd go to his officer then, and she would slip away. There would be some arrests perhaps, but no fighting because the mutiny would have been caught in the bud. Seamus would come home and she could shake off Father's shadow and be free to get on with her life.

The jolting motion of the trap irritated her so she flicked the reins. Immediately the jolting stopped and the trap took on a wave-like motion as Barney cantered. The hedges streamed past and Katie couldn't resist another slap with the reins.

'Feel that, Dafydd!' she yelled as the motion changed again, this time to a smooth, breath-taking flow. Barney had never galloped in the trap before. The wind whipped at Katie's hair, and she leant into the bend as the road swung to the left. 'Finn MacCool would have driven like this!' she called.

The fallen tree took her completely by surprise. She dragged on Barney's reins but he seemed unable to stop.

'Watch out, Dafydd!' But the barrier across the road grew and grew. Barney's chest was almost into the branches before they pulled up and she lost her footing. Terrified, Barney began to back. The trap was slewing to one side and in a second it would overturn. At that moment a soldier rose from the ditch and seized Barney's halter. The horse reared, but the soldier held him down.

'Where the hell do you think you're going!' roared a voice ahead of them. The branches quaked. Katie, tangled up in Dafydd's legs, struggled to get up off the floor. 'Hold them there, Corporal, don't let go.' An officer, Sam Brown belt shining, pushed into sight through the branches. His cap was knocked awry, one arm was in a sling and the other held a long-barrelled pistol which he raised and pointed at Katie. 'Stand up! Put your hands up. Who else have you got in there?' Dafydd appeared from the floor, pale and clearly shaken. 'You too; your hands where I can see them. Well? Who are you, and where are you going?'

'We're just doing messages, going into Nenagh,' said Katie, answering his last question first. 'I'm Katie O'Brien, this is Dafydd – he's from Wales, he doesn't speak English.' Why had she repeated that stupid lie?

'Messages? At the gallop?'

'What's happened?' she asked.

'What business is that of yours?' the officer snapped without lowering his pistol.

'None, none at all,' she stammered.

'I'll tell you what's bloody well happened.' Katie could see that his hand was shaking. She'd never seen anyone so angry before and was terrified the pistol would go off. 'A friend of mine, an officer, an Irishman – one of the best, one who fought with me against the English – has been shot dead in Nenagh by your so-called Republicans. They also shot Mrs O'Malley, a perfectly innocent by-stander, in the stomach, and she's died too. And then not ten minutes ago I got this from one of your friends when we came out to clear this tree.' He held up his bandaged hand. 'Now, where were you going at the gallop? Taking messages rather than doing them I'd say, or have they sent you to spy on us?'

'No, we just came round the corner and –'

'From now on we shoot on sight, and you can tell them that.'

'I ... we ... it's just the messages.'

'Well, stop looking all over the place for them!' The gun wobbled alarmingly. Katie *had* been looking, searching for a familiar face, but there were no friendly faces here. A group of soldiers in shirt sleeves stood idle but hostile, staring at them. A cross-cut saw emerged from the trunk of the tree, a neat pile of sawdust beneath it.

'Get on with your sawing there,' the officer shouted. He turned back to Katie. 'Well, are you spying? We used girls as spies often enough in the 'Tan war.' She shook her head. 'Corporal, do you know them?' he asked, turning to the soldier at Barney's head.

'Her father, O'Brien's all right, Sir; he was in the Great War, lost a hand. He's trying to reopen one of the slate quarries, I've heard. Her uncle up the hill, he'd be a Republican now. He was with us against the 'Tans.'

'What a mess!' said the officer. 'And now half of us are even wearing the same bloody uniforms! Back her off, corporal. You, girl, keep out of it. Go home where you belong, and stay there.' He turned on Dafydd and snapped, 'Where did she say you were from then? Come on, quickly.' Dafydd looked bewildered, shrugged his shoulders, and murmured something, presumably in Welsh. 'All right, off with you, and keep off the roads. They're not safe for children.'

*   *   *

Barney walked slowly, unurged. The foam from his gallop was

drying on his flanks. Katie was still shaking.

'Here, Frog, take the reins.' She put them into his hands. She had no comb, but running her fingers through her hair calmed her. She found a ribbon in her skirt pocket and tied her hair. 'Dafydd ... I'm sorry.' They were approaching the cross-roads again. 'Do you want to go home? It's not far, just up the hill the way we came.'

'Where are you going?'

'I need to think,' she said.

Dafydd hesitated. 'I'll be quiet.'

Katie turned Barney down the hill to the right towards the lake.

There was a patch of green beside the harbour. Katie hitched the reins so that Barney would not trip on them, and left him free. She led the way out on to the pier. The horse dropped his head gratefully and began to graze. The pier was deserted; coal and turf dust showed where a barge had been off-loaded. Jackdaws chattered in the ruins of the old castle that had once stood guard over the harbour. Ahead of them, Lough Derg spread out, a rippling sheet as far as the eye could see. Katie led the way down to a large slab of rock that sloped into the water. She sat there, gathering her skirts about her ankles. Dafydd sat down too, but at the far side of the slab. Water lapped softly with a rounded noise on the stones, the sound forming a background to Katie's silence.

'Frog,' she said after a while.

'Yes.'

'You're Welsh, aren't you?'

'Yes?' said Dafydd.

'If I talk to you in English you won't understand me will you?'

'Perhaps not. I haven't up to now anyway, have I?' He grinned.

'That was just a game. This is serious, deadly serious. And you won't remember what I say afterwards?'

'If I don't understand I can't, can I?'

Katie stared at the little waves as they raced in towards the shore. All she could see was the light reflected on their surfaces, then her eyes were drawn through the glitter to the honey-brown water-world below.

'It began when I went to meet Father at the station,' she said.

CHAPTER 8

Matches!

Secrets, Megan, are terrible things. Your twin brother is growing up fast. But why did she tell me? Why me? She has this game, see. Pretends I don't speak English – shuts me up, I suppose. At any rate, there she stood, her ragged skirt blowing and the waves of the Shannon dashing against her feet, and she told me everything. All the years she has nursed her father, silenced by the fear that he was mad, convinced he was a coward fleeing from some dreadful shame ...

* * *

'Father does not want me any more now,' said Katie as she finished her story. She gazed at the clouded sky while little waves dashed against the sloping stones at the edge of the lake. 'I gave him everything, Dafydd! I gave him my childhood, thinking he was sick, afraid he was mad. It didn't seem to matter that he was a coward or ashamed while he was sick. Now your Dad says it's just shell-shock and you, who never met him in your life before, can cure him with a word. "Angry" is all you said, and he was better. I don't know where I am, Dafydd. Is he sick, is he a coward, is he mad, or can't he face up to things because he ran away? Talk to me, Dafydd. Our game is over; I want to know.'

Out on the lake wind whipped at the water in front of an advancing storm. Katie took off her shoes and dipped her feet into the cool water. She thought of Barney and hoped there would be no thunder. Perhaps Dafydd had nothing to say. She looked down at him. He was folded up now, compact, legs crossed, looking out over the lake. She was surprised and a little frightened at the energy that seemed to be locked up inside him. 'Answer me, Dafydd!' she demanded.

'There is a story told among the Welsh miners who came back from the war of an Irishman who forgot his matches,' Dafydd began.

'What? ... Oh go on.'

'The Welsh were the miners in the war, see. The idea was to dig tunnels under the ground – secretly, like – until the tunnel was right under the German trenches. You dug out a room there and filled it with explosives. Then, just before a big attack you would set it off. Kill a lot of Germans, but chiefly it made a gap for the soldiers to get through.'

Katie shivered.

'Yes, it was horrible, but the Germans were doing it too. Dad talks of listening to them chattering away in their tunnel as they dug past in the opposite direction. Question of who got to the end first.'

'What happened if they met in the middle?'

'They bashed at each other with picks and shovels, hand to hand. Not nice. There was no-one in your Dad's tunnel when he found it though.'

'What do you mean?' asked Katie.

Dafydd looked up at her. 'He really told you *nothing* about all this?'

Katie stepped back out of the water and sat down, dropping her head on her knees. 'Just tell me!' she mumbled.

'One night an Irish sergeant was out on patrol in no-man's land when he and his men took shelter in a deep shell-hole quite close to a German machine-gun position. The soldiers hated that machine-gun but this was as close as they had ever managed to get to it. It had been raining and most of the shell holes had water in them, but this one was dry. Why was that? Where had the water gone to? the sergeant wondered. He crawled down, and there, to his surprise, was a hole; he wriggled into it. The shell had broken into a tunnel. It must have been one that the Germans had been digging towards the Irish trenches, but it was quite old. They must have abandoned it when the shell burst into it.

The sergeant could hardly believe his luck. In one direction it led straight towards the hated machine-gun, in the other it led back towards the Irish trenches. If they could tunnel in and find the end of the German tunnel from their own trenches they might be able to turn the tables on the Germans and blow that machine-gun sky high. That's when the sergeant asked for the Welsh miners to help.

'Dad had just finished a tunnel, a long deep one, at a place called Hill 60, when the news came that the Irish were being killed in hundreds by a machine-gun positioned on a little hill overlooking their trenches, but that they had found an old tunnel or something. Could the Welsh miners open it up? The soldiers called the place "Watch-it" after some Belgian village. Horrible place it was. The Germans were up on a hill and if anyone showed a whisker the machine-guns would swing on them. Cut through them like a scythe. There were three lines of trenches. Did your Dad tell you how it was?'

Katie nodded into her knees.

Dafydd went on. 'They were joined by communication trenches. Dad was warned as he went up that the Irish were all Sinn Féiners and would run away as soon as fight, but he had heard the same said about the Welsh running away, so he didn't take any notice.

'The sergeant who had had the idea of mining the machine-gun position was a chap called O'Brien.' Katie looked up; she'd wondered if it was Father. 'Well, Dad and he got on fine, both had been in slate-quarrying, see. They planned the tunnel together. It had to intersect with the end of the German tunnel, also it had to be done quickly as there was a big attack planned. Usually the Welsh were left to themselves to do the tunnelling, but Sergeant O'Brien could get his men to do anything. He had refused a commission just so he could stay with his men and they loved him for it. So there was a steady stream of Irish volunteers to help.

'It wasn't easy tunnelling. Then they had to repair places where the tunnel had collapsed. Eventually the day came when Dad knew they were under the German machine-gun position. They could hear it firing above them. The explosives were packed into the end of the tunnel, and only just in time too because the order came that they were to go over the top, machine-guns or no machine-guns, for a big attack that very night. Usually the explosion would be set off using an electrical wire, but O'Brien was old-fashioned and he said he didn't trust this wire, not when the lives of his men were at risk, so he asked for a back-up fuse, the sort you light with a match but which burns faster than you can walk. Dad agreed, and begged some from the engineers – "sappers" they called them.

71

'The attack was to take place just before dawn. Dad was all right, he would not have to go over the top. His job would be done when the mine blew. Not so O'Brien. He was just a sergeant, but the officers were young and inexperienced, so he would lead the men over the top himself. Dad watched him getting them ready, talking to the them like they were all old friends, children almost, checking that they had everything, collecting letters to their loved ones. It was real quiet. They stopped for a moment and listened to a nightingale singing in the stump of a wood a little way off. Dad talks of that quiet like it was some gift from God. I think myself God had gone away and left them. Everything was ready. The big guns of the artillery would start by shooting shells into the German trenches, then Dad would blow the mine and, while the German machine-guns were silenced, O'Brien would lead the attack over no-man's land and take the German trenches. That was the plan at any rate.

'Then disaster struck. Dad says he can hear the scream of that shell to this day. It was one of ours, meant for the German trenches, but it fell short. A huge column of mud and dirt shot up exactly where the tunnel lay. Immediately the German machine-gunners woke up and started to fire. Dad pressed the plunger to explode the mine but nothing happened. He lit the fuse and they watched the flame rush off into the tunnel. Himself and your dad counted how long it would take, but nothing happened. The shell must have burst into the tunnel and cut both the wire and the fuse. "I don't believe it!" Dad shouted over the din. "A shell has cut the tunnel a second time! There is nothing we can do."

'O'Brien went mad then. It was just minutes before he would have to take his men over the lip of the trench and the machine-guns were going wild. Above their heads there was a singing hail of bullets. O'Brien knew that not one man in ten would survive the first ten seconds of the attack.

'"I'm going to set it off myself!" he yelled.

'"You can't," shouted Dad. "The tunnel's been cut by that shell!"

'"Yes I can. There's still that shell-hole where we discovered the tunnel first. Remember, you left an opening for air."

'"But you'll be blown up with the mine. It's just under the machine-guns, you'll never get there!"

'Your Dad never replied. Dead against orders it was, but he was over the top in a flash. Bullets swept over the parapet like angry bees. Dad didn't even dare to put his head up, then suddenly O'Brien was back, falling down into the trench. They rushed to help him. No wonder he had run back. No one could face fire like that alone.'

Katie looked out over the bleak water – poor Father, poor, poor Father.

Dafydd had gone husky and cleared his throat. 'But he hadn't given up, Katie. "Matches," he was yelling. "I forgot my matches." Dad couldn't believe it; he meant to go up there *again*? But he pulled out a box and gave it to him. Your father thrust his rifle at Dad. "I won't need that," he shouted. Then he signalled to two of his men to help him; they seemed to know at once what he wanted. Like lifting a man on to a horse they literally threw him up and over. Dad leapt up on to the firing platform to see. It was foolish; everyone else had their heads down because at that moment the Germans sent up a flare – lit up the whole place it did. Our mad Irishman was in the middle of no-man's land streaking across the open ground like a hare, not even dropping into shell-holes for cover. Perhaps the flare blinded the German machine-gunners because it seemed impossible that anyone could survive that firing.

Then the running figure disappeared seemingly under the barrels of the machine-guns. At least he was sheltered there. Someone was pulling at Dad's trousers to get him to come down. The men were ready to go over. At that moment Dad saw a movement in the shell-hole. A hand appeared, waving. Could it be a signal? Then the hand was gone. A sheet of flame shot skywards from the German machine-gun position and my Dad was pulled off the ledge as the Irish went over the top.

'It was the Welsh miners that dug your father out. They did not take kindly to going into no-man's land, not after weeks of mining, but they did it for Sergeant O'Brien. He was half-buried in the blast from the mine. Dad remembers him on the stretcher on the way to hospital. "I tried to signal," he said, "but they shot my bloody hand off."' Dafydd stopped. 'O'Brien got a medal for it too – the Military Medal. Did he ever tell you?'

Katie sat in a daze. Could this really be the same story that Father had told her all those years ago up at the Graves of the Leinstermen? Where was the running away? Running into the fighting he was instead. And where was the terror? But it was the same story. It most gloriously was! She stood up unsteadily. A few huge drops of rain splashed on the rock between the two of them. The cloud which had bent over them like a black bat swept past and a shaft of vivid sunlight lit the rock from the south. Out on the lake the water foamed white where the rain lashed its surface. Katie could hear the hiss of the shower on the water as it passed them by. Stunned, she picked up her shoes.

'We'd better be getting back,' she said, hardly trusting her voice. She helped Dafydd to his feet as if in a dream. They climbed back up the harbour wall. Barney glanced up and whinnied. Katie turned to look back over the lake. Crowned in white, the black cloud stood low over the water, propped up, it seemed, by the stump of a rainbow so bright, so vivid, it made her gasp.

CHAPTER 9

Hidden Arms

Dafydd remained silent as they climbed up into the trap and started on the road home. He avoided her eyes. Katie looked at him with appreciation and was grateful. When they reached the cross-roads she turned right up the steep hill into the village of Portroe. She hitched Barney to a ring in the wall and they went into the shop. It smelled of brown paper, stale bread and porter. She liked the smell. She bought two pounds of sugar, some cards of grey darning wool and, with her own money, a quarter pound of bullseyes.

Mrs Gleeson thumped the bag of sugar on the counter till it settled, bound it with twine, and wrote the messages into the book for Father to pay later. No, she told them, the *Nenagh Guardian* had not come in nor the *Independent* either.

But, and she lowered her voice, had Katie heard that *they* had felled a tree right across the road not two miles down the road? The way she said 'they' made Katie wonder if Mrs Gleeson wasn't rather pleased. It felt strange that she no longer knew what someone in her own village was thinking. She backed towards the door, avoiding sacks of hen feed and the blue crystals used to spray potatoes. She didn't want to talk about the tree; there might be questions.

*   *   *

'I could learn to type and keep his books,' she said without warning as Barney plodded up the hill. Dafydd looked so surprised Katie thought he had swallowed his bullseye.

'Where? On the farm?' he asked.

'No, you mutt. When the quarry opens.'

Dafydd took his bullseye out and examined it to see if the stripes went right through.

Katie went on defensively. 'I can't do sums, but I'm sure I could if I had to.'

'I thought you wanted to lead a revolution,' said Dafydd, popping the sweet back in.

'Bad Frog! Don't tease me. I must settle down, go to the nuns.'

This time Dafydd really did look startled. 'Nuns! Become ... become a *nun*?'

'No! Secondary school, the Sisters of Mercy in Nenagh next year. Perhaps they have typing classes.'

'I can't imagine you as a nun.'

Katie ignored that. 'Father's right, what Ireland needs is economic development.'

'Long words!'

'They're Father's, but he's right. We'll get the quarry going and then there will be lots of jobs and money for people to spend.'

'What about stopping the war?'

'I don't seem to be very good at that, do I? If everyone had jobs they wouldn't bother. You'll see, the men will come up tomorrow and your Dad will tell us how to get started. We could be up and running by the end of the summer. The fighting will be over by then and we can throw our guns into the lake and have done with them for ever.'

*   *   *

Peter was waiting anxiously when they drove into the yard.

'I thought you'd never come. I should never have let you go. Your Dad will skin me.' He ran his finger along the line of dried

76

foam on Barney's flank. 'Will you look at the lather you have on him.'

'He was a bit fresh,' said Katie, climbing down. 'We went down to Garrykennedy. Would you have had us walk?'

'It would have done you no harm at all,' Peter said as he unhooked the trap. 'Hold Barney there now,' he said, and rolled the trap in under the shed. 'Now, let's get him out of sight.' Katie led the horse into the stable while Peter followed, grumbling.

'I bought you some bullseyes. There's nearly a quarter there. Dafydd and I had one each on the way up.'

'You're a good girl,' said Peter, pocketing the paper bag. 'Just give me a hand with rubbing Barney down now. There's no need for him to look like he was at the races.' Peter hissed soothingly through his teeth as they worked away with handfuls of hay until he shone.'

'I'm going to learn to type, Peter,' said Katie conversationally. 'Won't that be grand.'

'Like a secretary? And what would you want to do that for?' Peter, who groomed Barney just as he milked the cows, with his head against the animal's flank, straightened up and pushed his cap back on his head.

'To help Father with the quarry when it opens.'

'That'll be the day.'

'What do you mean?' asked Katie indignantly.

'He's looking for money from people. What they want is to be paid.'

'But that's how a co-operative works. Everyone chips in a little and then you share out the profits.'

'It's not for me to say.' Barney shifted uneasily. 'Whoah there, Barney or I'll make meat of you. Anyway, they have other things on their minds, old grudges.'

'You mean Father going to the war?'

'Could be.'

'That's stupid! Father'll win them over. You'll see.'

Peter chuckled. 'And you learning to type, that'll be the day.'

Katie threw her screw of hay at him and skipped out.

* * *

There was work to be done in the house after dinner. Marty took Dafydd and a couple of hurleys down to the flat field where his friends were playing. Katie wanted to tell her mother about her plans, but Mother was distracted – worried about Seamus perhaps, so Katie decided not to mention the felled tree or her little brush with the army. Father and Mr Parry did not come back till late having walked over to see some of the old slate quarries down by the Shannon. Katie went to bed early feeling more at peace with herself than she had in years.

* * *

Frantic tapping at her door woke her. It was quite dark.

'Yes?' she said, fumbling for matches. There followed an unintelligible mumble. 'Come in!' she called in irritation. The door opened a crack and Dafydd's head appeared. He was carrying a candle at a dangerous angle. 'For God's sake, Frog, watch that candle. What's the matter?'

'Seamus is back,' he whispered hoarsely. 'He's hurt.' In a second Katie was out of bed and across the room, snatching the candle from Dafydd.

'Look!' he said as he retreated in front of her, pointing to a dark spot on the floor, 'that's blood.' Without knocking, Katie opened the door of the boys' bedroom. There was sudden movement from the direction of Seamus's bed where he appeared to be tucking in the blankets.

'What's the matter, Seamus? Are you hurt?' she said, relieved that he wasn't prostrate on the bed. He turned and sat down on it. He looked pale, but he was smiling, and there was a bright spark of excitement in his eyes.

'Keep your voice down,' she warned. 'If you're not dying don't raise the house.'

'I'm fine,' he said, but he swayed a little.

'No you're not, you're bleeding. Let me look at you.'

'It's just a scratch ... I think.'

'Hold this, Frog,' said Katie, thrusting the candle at Dafydd. 'Where?' she demanded. 'Where does it hurt?'

'Across my back and shoulder.'

'Turn round.' Katie could see a ragged tear in the shirt. 'You'll have to take your shirt off.'

'Ouch, it's stuck.'

'I'll get some hot water.' She took the candle from Dafydd and went downstairs. She was anxious, and that made her cross. If only she could call Father – he knew about wounds – but that was out of the question. Things were bad enough between him and Seamus. She filled a basin with hot water from the kettle at the back of the range, and got iodine, cotton-wool, lint, a bandage and some sticking plaster from the cupboard under the stairs.

'This will hurt,' she said grimly as she dabbed at the wound with iodine. She had got it as clean as she could without starting it bleeding again. She had been relieved to find that the cut was not too deep. The iodine made a dark stain, and had a sharp smell. Seamus drew his breath in sharply.

'Ouch!'

'I told you.' Only the deeper cut on his shoulder was still bleeding. She bandaged this tightly.

'Does it look like a bullet wound?' he asked.

'It's very ragged.'

'Probably a ricochet,' he said with satisfaction.

'What happened?' Katie asked as she eased his night-shirt over his head.

'We were fired on. Katie, it was so exciting! After all these years of waiting and wanting to be in action, then I was, and I managed!'

'What did you manage?'

'You remember the mutiny I was telling you would happen in Nenagh? Well, on Friday the lads from the Kenyon Street barracks came out on our side and took over the whole town and occupied the post office –'

'Yes, and shot poor Mrs O'Malley in the process.'

'How do you know about that? We don't know who shot Mrs O'Malley. She was standing in her porch, which was silly.'

'There was a soldier shot too.'

'Who's been telling you all this? That was a Free State officer, when they took over the Hibernian Hotel.'

'But why, Seamus? What was it all for?'

'Listen to me,' he dropped his voice, 'during the fuss, the lads got away with whole a load of guns and ammunition from the barracks, that's why! They had them covered up in a cart and were escaping out of town when the horse went lame. They knew the government troops would be after them and were desperate to find somewhere to hide the stuff. So they took the first farm they came to and hid cart and all in a barn. They told the farmer he'd be shot if he breathed a word about it, and took to the fields. That was Friday.'

Marty stirred, asked what was going on, but went back to sleep again before any of them could answer. Katie sat down on the edge of the bed. Seamus's eyes glinted in the light of the candle Dafydd was holding. She knew he wanted to talk, and she wanted to know. Outside the circle of candlelight the whole house was quiet.

'Go on,' she said.

'Well, yesterday, when the lads had pulled out of the town, one of the girls in Nenagh who knew where the stuff was hidden happened to see the farmer in question hovering about the police barracks. She put two and two together and went up to him and asked about his health and remarked on the sad shortness of life. He went away in a hurry then, but it was decided that the stuff would have to be moved at once, and our column was called on to do it!

'Katie, it was beautiful to see how it was all organised. A group of the lads were sent off to cut through a tree ready to drop behind us if we were followed. The rest of us requisitioned a horse and hied us off down the road to the farm. There was a light upstairs, and someone in the farm moved the curtains, but no-one came out. It was just getting dark – perfect timing – and we were harnessed up when all at once there was a clatter like forty tin cans on the road and there was this girl from the town on an ancient bicycle she'd grabbed that had no front tyre.

'"They're coming!" she said, "You've got twenty minutes at the most." The old fellow must have split on us after all. That set us hopping like fleas, I can tell you, but the horse was fresh. Twenty minutes seemed a fair margin.'

'Did you shoot the farmer?'

'Never gave it a thought. We had to get going, but I bet he'll have some sleepless nights for a while.

'We were cracking on, taking turns on the shaft, or running behind, when disaster struck. I felt the gust of wind myself, just before we heard the crash. You see, the lads had the tree cut through, and left it held up by a whisker. They said later they could actually hear us on the road and were ready to give

81

a cheer, when one of those blessed night gusts that blows on to the lake, took the tree. One eejit even tried to hold it back and nearly got squashed. As I said, we heard the crash, and when we arrived there it was across the road. And the government troops expected behind us!' Seamus paused. 'Would you ever get me some water?'

'Dafydd, take the candle,' said Katie. 'And miss out the second-last step before the landing; it creaks. The spring water is in the enamel bucket in the porch.' Katie waited until he was gone. 'Seamus, have you thought? Those rifles and bullets were made to kill people?'

'I'm not a barbarian, Katie, I have been thinking of that. But if we don't throw the English out *now*, and completely, there will be fighting in Ireland until they're gone. Mark my words, there's a passion out there that nothing will quench.'

Katie could feel that passion in his voice and it frightened her. 'But it's not even the English you're fighting now, it's us. If there were no guns we could get on with living.'

'The guns would just come from somewhere else.'

'But still, one bullet less, one life more.'

The stair creaked. Dafydd had forgotten the loose step on the way up. The wavering light approached, then they heard a door open.

'Shhh!' Katie hissed, and held her breath.

'Is everything all right there?' came Father's voice. Katie's tongue seemed stuck to her mouth.

'Sorry, Mr O'Brien, I was getting a glass of water.'

'Oh! all right, Dafydd, sleep well.' They all breathed again.

'Father must know *nothing*, Seamus!' Katie whispered as Seamus drank.

'That's better,' he said with a sigh. 'I shouldn't be talking to you either.'

'What did you do then?' Katie was anxious that he shouldn't stop.

'For a while there was pandemonium, everyone blaming everyone else, then the commandant got us sorted out – you saw him, the man up at Uncle Mal's. Josie was to take the horse and find a way around through the fields if he could. The rest of us were to unload the cart. You've never felt anything so heavy as an ammunition box, Katie. There was a big machine-gun too, a beauty, with shining ammunition in belts. When it was all over we got everyone pulling and lifting and pushing until somehow we got the empty cart over the tree.

'Then we had to load it up again. I was staggering with exhaustion before we got the last box on board. Suddenly the commandant told us to shush. The government troops were coming; we could hear their boots like hail on the road, and we still had no horse. A couple of the lads got behind the tree with rifles to slow them down, then we all threw ourselves at the cart. But it was too late, they could see us and they started shooting.'

'Did they get them, the guns I mean?'

'No, but nearly. Stars give an awful lot of light when you don't want them to. I heard one bullet hit the road behind us and go singing off into the trees. Next I got a crack across the shoulder like Satan's whip. It didn't hurt so much as burn. I wanted to stop, but the commandant was calling for me – we had to get off the main road and I was to show them the way, so I just had to put up with it.'

'Did Josie get through?' asked Katie.

'Yes, we met him a few minutes later saying he had been holding back in case the horse was hit. The lads had a thing or two to say about that but the commandant said how he was right as we'd never pull the cart all the way by ourselves.

We left the main road then.'

'Where did you bring them?' asked Katie.

'I was told not to say.'

'But you've got to. Where?'

'I'm tired, Katie.'

'Was it to Uncle Mal's? They know he's a Republican, they'll be up there after him.'

'Look, Katie, forget it.'

'But, Seamus, we've got to destroy them! Think of all the lives we can save.'

'Are you mad, Katie? I thought you were on our side. You wanted to join me, you said so. You came all the way up to Uncle Mal's.'

'I was fed up with Father then, but I think he's right now. Guns have no place in Ireland. Did you know that he has the Military Medal for bravery, Seamus? But he wouldn't boast about it because he hates guns and war. And he's right, Seamus. Can't you see? You've got the guns and ammunition away from the army – well done, but that's enough. Let's destroy them, throw them in the Shannon, then they can't kill anybody.'

Seamus looked stunned. 'You wouldn't ... I mean ... tell what I've told you? I ... I thought ...'

Katie thought hard for a moment and then said. 'No, Seamus, I'm not going to be an informer now, and neither is Dafydd. Who would we tell that wouldn't use the guns if they had them anyway? But don't ask me not to look. Lie back now, you need a rest.'

As Katie turned to close the door of her room she looked back at Dafydd. He was sitting up in bed still holding the candle, his eyes like saucers. What did he make of all this?

She did not go to sleep immediately but knelt on her window ledge looking out, breathing in the sharp night air. The moon had risen; under its light she noticed a mouse run out from the shed, work busily at the hen-feed that had lodged between the stones, and then dart back to safety. She wanted to worry about Seamus but the worry would not come. All she could think of was Father, how brave he had been and how wrong she had been about him. Perhaps she nodded off for a moment because she had a sudden vision of Dafydd and Father walking towards her. Father was laughing and holding back, but Dafydd was pulling him by his good arm. Dear Dafydd, she thought. She hesitated for a second before sliding gratefully into bed – would she wake him and thank him now? No ... she'd leave that till the morning.

CHAPTER 10

The Royal Court

Katie woke to world of magic. Father's all right, she thought. Her whole room seemed to be suffused with a special light. She found herself looking in wonder at the wallpaper. It was just ordinary wallpaper with sprigs of tiny blue forget-me-nots and scarlet pimpernel clinging to a paper trellis, but today they looked real. She wanted to reach out and touch the delicate petals. 'Father's all right!' she kept repeating to herself. She thought of the lapping waves of the Shannon at her feet and heard Dafydd's lilting voice telling her Father's story, the true story. She'd believed in Father before because she had loved him, not because he was a hero, a real live hero of her own. She got up carefully, so as not to shatter her mood, walked over to her wash-stand, poured water into the basin and watched the painted roses sway in the swirling water.

When she had washed she sat on the edge of her bed with her face in her towel and let it all sink in. Life would begin for her again today. The quarry men would climb the hill, as she could remember them doing before the war, and Father's dream of reopening the quarry would come true. She would be his right-hand – no, he still had his right hand – his left-hand person, his secretary, look after his books and learn to use a typewriter. One day, when they were alone, she would tell him that Dafydd had told her all about his medal and how brave he had been.

She loved everybody this morning. Spreading out both arms she imagined that if she could just stretch out far enough she could gather them all in together: Mother, Marty, Seamus, Father, the soldier boy from Nenagh, Mr Parry, even Dafydd, no, specially Dafydd, and pull them all in to her. Then, just as she imagined drawing them all in, she remembered the guns. It came as a start. Where had Seamus hidden the guns? How could she pull everyone together when the guns bristled between them like a twig of thorns.

'Damn,' she said, 'damn!' A thrush which had been repeating its song with variations in the sycamore below the barn, flew away.

*　　*　　*

'You're coming into the pew with us, Eamonn O'Brien, like a respectable citizen,' said Mother, taking Father firmly by the arm. 'No shuffling with the men at the back. If Father MacDonagh is going to make an announcement I want you in a pew.' Father made a wry face which made him look absurdly like Marty. Katie slipped into the pew where she could sit beside him. She breathed the moth-ball smell off his Sunday suit and enjoyed his closeness.

'*In nómine Patris, et Filii, et Spiritus Sancti. Amen,*' said the priest.

'*Introibo et altáre Dei. Ad Deum qui lætificat juventútem meam,*' came the piping response from the altar boys. Katie knew the responses by heart from helping Marty to learn them during his brief and undistinguished career as an altar boy. Katie always started Mass by trying to translate the Latin words. Today, however, she did not struggle to understand them, instead she let them take on shapes.

'*Gloria in excélsis Deo.*
Et in terra pax homínibus
bonæ voluntátis.
Laudámus ...'

Each shape slipped down inside her until it fitted into some special place for it within her soul.

She emerged reluctantly from her trance when Fr Mac-Donagh began his sermon. He was old and thin and had an Adam's apple that did surprising things as he talked. He had an old-fashioned way of speaking.

'There are those who would turn the guns of our new-found freedom against the soldiers of our own country,' he began. Katie wondered where Seamus was. Neither she nor Dafydd (bless him) had said anything about the night's happenings at breakfast. Now, if she were Seamus, she wondered, where would she hide a cartload of arms?

Marty was nudging her. She looked up. Fr MacDonagh was looking straight at Father.

'But there is one who is trying to bring life back to our hills by providing gainful employment where, since the war in Europe, only goats and rough cattle have grazed.' The priest looked a bit like a goat himself. Marty's subdued bleat, 'Ma-hahah,' came out louder than he intended. Katie gave him a dig in the ribs.

'If there are true patriots among you, take the slater's hammer in preference to the gun and go today to O'Brien's quarry where I am told there will be a meeting to discuss the reopening of the quarry and so to restart this ancient craft again in Ireland.' Katie gave her father's arm a squeeze and pressed her head against his shoulder. She wanted to stand up in church and shout out to everybody how her father was the best and bravest man in Ireland. She felt in her pocket; she still had a penny. She would light a candle for his quarry – no – for *their* quarry, on the way out.

*   *   *

Barney's head bobbed into the hill and his hooves slipped where the bare rock emerged through the worn surface of the road. Katie could hear singing somewhere on the hillside above the farm. She turned to listen to Father. He had moved over in the trap to sit beside Mother; his arm was around her shoulders.

'Mary ... but to give us half his sermon!' he was exclaiming. 'I only expected a mention among the church notices. They'll come flocking now. Griffith is adamant that the old quarry isn't safe, but he has it all planned for me. You know how the previous owner dumped the waste slate in a huge pile above the quarry?'

'They say he was too mean to put the waste on his good fields,' said Mother. 'I've always been worried that it might slip down on top of you.'

'Well, Griffith says let it slip. The best of the slate is covered by that tip. Push the waste down into the old quarry and start again in fresh rock, he says.'

'Won't that cost the earth?'

'Not what you think. It's all downhill. Griff says that with a little money, or even free labour, we could have it down by autumn.'

'Will the men do that? Work just for the promise of a job?'

'It's more than a promise. We'll make it a co-operative. That means the men will have a share in the profits when it gets going. We could be producing by this time next year, just think!'

'I hope you're right, dear. People are slow to part with their money and they have other things on their minds just now.'

'Don't be such a wet blanket, Mother,' laughed Katie, and the house came into view. High on the hill Dafydd was singing, then Mr Parry's voice came in below him. She recognised the tune; it was one father whistled sometimes.

'Will you listen to those two sing,' said Mother. 'Mr Parry says the boy wants to leave school to work in the quarries. I'd say that lad had more brain than brawn.'

'Well, they're at odds, so. Griff really wants Dafydd to stay on in school and bring his brains to the quarries if he wants to later.'

Katie smiled to herself. She was pleased with her Frog. He was doing well. He'd said nothing about wanting to work in the quarries, but that wasn't her business.

*   *   *

The men arrived at the quarry yard in ones and twos, still in their Sunday suits, pushing bicycles or walking over the fields, following paths not trodden since the quarries closed at the start of the Great War eight years before.

Katie took up position on the spoil-heap which curved around one end of it, and from here she had a bird's eye view of the gathering. Much further down, to her left, the quarry gaped like an open grave, dissolving into black shadow. Uphill, enclosing the quarry on three sides, was a horse-shoe shaped pile of broken slate which seemed to lean in and threaten the dark hole below. So this was the pile that Father and Mr Parry wanted to shovel down! It looked an impossible task. On the rim of the black hole was a broad ledge which was the quarry yard, a flat area where, in the old days, the rough blocks of slate which had been lifted out of the quarry, were trimmed and split to make slates for people to put on their roofs. In recent years Father had stacked hay there and used the derelict sheds to store potatoes, but it was empty now and the men were gathering there. The rusty cables, which had once been used to lift blocks of slate up out of the quarry floor to the yard still spanned the hole beside them.

Beyond the yard was the cut, a steep-sided ravine sliced at right angles to the quarry in order to let the water out. It always gave Katie the shivers. Father had explained how, as the quarry got deeper and deeper, the men had had to make the cut deeper too. It let the water run out, but it also made it possible for them to walk into the quarry floor to work – if they didn't want to swing down in a bucket. Katie could just see the top of it. There was a man standing there on the far side of it wearing a trench coat and, like her, watching the gathering. She wondered idly what he was doing there.

She looked back to where Father, Mr Parry and Dafydd stood together. The rest of the men were hanging back, talking among themselves, picking up bits of slate and weighing them in their hands and then throwing them back on the spoil. Who were they waiting for?

She turned to her right towards where the farm nestled in its sheltering belt of sycamore trees. The road to the quarry ran behind the farm. Along this an ancient gnome of a man was advancing, so bandy-legged that Katie thought he'd be more comfortable sitting on a barrel than on a chair. This was Paddy Scully. He was wearing his Sunday suit. As she looked, he stopped, mopped his head with a large blue handkerchief, and straightened his jacket and cap with care. Then, like an actor taking the stage, he walked on to the quarry yard. The men closed in behind him. Katie watched as Father came forward and shook hands, then she got up and clattered down the slate pile to join the gathering.

She looked for Dafydd as she edged into the crowd, but could not see him. Then she found a block of stone to stand on and stretched to see over the heads of the men. Father had propped a line of slates of all sizes against the wall of the shed and old Paddy Scully was walking down the line.

'There you are,' Paddy said loudly, 'the Royal Court.' He tapped the largest of the slates. 'You, boy, what's that one called?'

Katie saw Dafydd as he stepped forward. Would he pretend he didn't understand? To her relief he said in English, 'It's a Queen, Sir. A heavy Queen.' Katie knew how heavy those huge slates were.

'Heavy, my foot! It's a Queen, an Irish Queen, none of your Welsh wafers here. Look at them, all my pretty ladies: Princess, Duchess, Countess, Ladies, Doubles, Mosses, Quarters and Commons. You see, the old fool hasn't forgotten his slates.'

'Indeed, I know you haven't,' said Father. 'Come here, Paddy, and show Mr Parry you can still split one too. I have it all set up here for you.'

'Of course I can split a slate,' snorted the old man, but he eyed the roughly-squared block of stone carefully. Then he straddled the bench, took the flat-bladed chisel that Father had left handy, tested its edge and picked up the wooden mallet.

Katie remembered Mick-the-Shilling's demonstration. 'This was a good mallet once,' the old man said grudgingly, 'cut from a crab tree, it was.'

'Like yerself, you old grumbler – get on with it,' murmured one of the men beside her. Katie smiled. Carefully the old quarry-man eyed the grain of the rock. Then he took the chisel and began to open up a split close to one face. The block was large so he took the split down its sides as well. Katie half-wished the slate would crack, but it didn't. With a final tap, a perfect slate slipped off the face of the slab, and there was a murmur of approval from the watchers. But the old man was scowling.

'What sort of a block is that, Eamonn O'Brien? Would you shame me? The sap's gone out of it. I know what you're at. You're trying to trick me into making a good slate from bad stone! That block is rubbish. Quarrying up here at the surface of the hill is no good. No good at all. I'll show you where the good slate is. Come with me.'

Throwing down his tools he lurched towards the quarry edge. The men parted to let him through. Katie followed. When she got to the quarry rim she held on tightly to one of the rusty cables before peering down. Paddy Scully was pointing to the bottom of the quarry floor. It seemed miles down. 'There she is! Down there at the very bottom, as sweet a vein of slate as you ever saw.'

'But, Paddy, the walls are too steep. There's a danger of a fall,' said Father. 'Our plan is –'

'Stuff and nonsense! What sort of men are you? This is the safest quarry in Tipperary. Can't you walk out from the bottom through the cut if a fall is going to happen?'

'But how can you know when a fall is about to take place? The rocks don't tell you!' asked Mr Parry incredulously.

'But the goats do, the goats do!' said the old man triumphantly.

'Goats?'

'Yes, goats. They live all over the tips above the quarry. If a fall is going to happen, after heavy rain maybe, the goats go off up the mountain. They know. All we do is keep an eye on the goats! We weren't too scared to work down there before, why should you be now? The sweetest slate is there and with the sap in it too.'

So that was old Paddy's line – rely on the goats to give a warning so the men could escape out through the cut. Katie knew Father would never agree to that. It was just too risky. There would be a lot of talk before Father would persuade Paddy though – and the men would follow Paddy. The talk was getting technical: safe angles of slope, faults and joints. Also, Katie was feeling uneasy. It wasn't just the drop at her feet, it was the feeling of being watched. She scanned the hill above and then turned towards the cut. She stiffened. The man in the trench coat was still there. What is more, at that moment he lowered the pair of field-glasses he'd been watching them with and turned. Katie stood riveted. Where she had seen that coat before? He began to climb the hill, a black dog trotting at his heels. Then it all came back: at Uncle Mal's – and the dog had been in the barn. A second man appeared beside the first and she turned to look at him. As she watched he turned too and she saw his profile clearly; it was Seamus! Now, what was Seamus doing there, she wondered, with a stab of resentment. Seamus should be here helping Father, and not ... but a new thought struck her ... where were the guns? Was it possible they were somewhere nearby?

Mr Parry was describing in detail how the quarry could be

made safe and a new start made, but Katie's mind was racing. There *was* a place, a secret place, that she and Seamus both knew about where things could be hidden. The quarry would keep. Those guns were like a thorn in her side now. Where was Dafydd?

CHAPTER 11

Gunpowder

Dafydd was standing at the quarry edge, his mouth open in amazement. Katie pulled him back, afraid he might absent-mindedly walk into the abyss.

'What are you doing – catching flies?' she laughed.

'Goats!' he said huskily. 'Goats, Katie! Is he mad?'

'No, it's a fact.' Katie couldn't help laughing. 'Come on, I'll show you.' She grabbed him by the arm. She wanted to see where the man in the trench coat was going, but Dafydd hesitated.

'Maybe I should stay with Dad? What are they talking about now?'

'Flying pigs perhaps,' said Katie, remembering guiltily that Dafydd wanted to be a quarry-man. But she wanted him with her. 'Come on, I want you to come with me, I'll show you the goats.' She led the way around the end of the quarry and up on to the slippery pile of waste slate. '*Sligins*, we call them,' she panted over her shoulder.

They reached the crest of the tip-heap above the quarry, where there were the remains of a narrow-gauge railway, with wobbly lines and rotten sleepers. A steep little valley, filled with trees and bushes, was hidden between the tip-heap and the open mountain behind. Katie scanned the valley and the mountain slope; there was no sign of the man in the trench coat. Could he be in the trees?

'The goats are usually in here,' she said as she skated down the slope and ducked into a goat-sized green tunnel through the bushes. She could hear Dafydd following behind. There was a strong smell of goat and the path was soft with droppings. She had pressed on past some rocks, when a stifled exclamation came from behind her. She turned, and Dafydd was pointing up the rocky crag beside them, his eyes popping, to where, looking down at him, was an enormous billy goat, his chinaman's beard tucked into his chest.

'Will he attack?' Dafydd whispered.

'Of course not,' Katie replied hopefully. 'We'll just walk on quietly. You're lucky,' she said over her shoulder. 'That's the king of the goats. Usually all you see is old nanny goats.' There was no reply. She turned, but Dafydd seemed to be on his knees worshipping the goat, his head in a crack in the ground.

'Come on,' she called. 'He's not an idol! And he may not be idle either.' She was anxious, and in awe of the huge goat which was looking down at Dafydd curiously. She wanted to get on and the paths seemed to have changed since she and Seamus used to come up here. She ducked into one of the green tunnels. Dafydd was saying something but it was too narrow and prickly to turn, so she pressed on. After a while she found a place where she could stand up and cast about her, to get her bearings. Dafydd caught up.

'Katie –' he began.

'There's a little house in here somewhere which Seamus and I found years ago,' she interrupted. 'It's where the young goats gather. I thought you'd like to see it. We weren't able to get into it then, perhaps we could now.'

'I ought to tell Dad about that crack, where the goat was.'

'Oh, I thought you were praying to him. Do that later. There's cracks everywhere. Let's keep quiet while I see if I can find the place.'

The house, when she found it, was little more than a shed deeply buried in brambles. The goats, however, had opened tunnel-paths into it and there was an open space about the front door. It was a lot smaller than she had remembered and there were no goats there now. Neither was there any sign of the man in the trench coat. The walls of the house were made of huge blocks of slate and great slabs formed the roof. Katie wondered why it had been made so strong, like a small fortress. The door was made of iron and was held in place by a rusty padlock. She examined this carefully, disappointed that it was rusted up; it hadn't been opened for years. There were no arms here.

Dafydd emerged from the bushes, looked at the house and said, 'I know what that is.' But Katie didn't reply. She was looking for a stone to hit the padlock with.

'This should do it,' she said.

Dafydd looked up as she raised the stone.

'Stop!' he yelled in alarm, but he was too late. With a clang like a church bell the padlock spun off into the bushes. Katie lost her grip on the stone and jumped back as it crashed at her feet.

'Why stop?' she said. 'Look, that was a wallop for you!'

'Just don't hit anything else,' pleaded Dafydd. 'I'm taking my boots off.'

Katie, puzzled, laughed and said, 'You've been a good Frog today. You may keep your boots on.'

'You don't know what you nearly did!' said Dafydd as he

struggled with his laces. 'That's a magazine.'

'Like the *Illustrated London News*?'

'No, Miss O'Brien, not a picture magazine but a magazine that goes bang when girls hit it with stones. It's a store where they kept gunpowder for the old quarry. Nobody is allowed to wear nailed boots, or carry matches or smoke, or hit things with huge rocks, in case they make a spark and blow everybody up.'

'I bet there's no powder in there now. Let's look.'

'Should we?'

'Why not? It's Father's now anyway.' Katie waited while Dafydd picked his way fastidiously through the goat droppings. The hinges squeaked and sprinkled them with rust as they pushed the door in. It was pitch dark inside.

'I wish we had a candle,' said Katie.

'No you don't,' reminded Dafydd. Slowly their eyes adjusted to the dark. The shed was disappointingly empty. Some wooden boxes were aligned along one wall, one of which contained what looked like a spool of rope. There was a heap of sacks against the far wall. Katie pulled at these, then jumped back.

'Spiders!' she said in disgust.

Dafydd came forward. 'There's a barrel under here.' He tipped the sacks off in a cloud of dust.

'Careful, those spiders look explosive,' said Katie.

The barrel had a wooden lid. Dafydd lifted this off and peered in. He dipped in his hand. 'It's half-full,' he said.

'Half-full of what?'

'I don't know – feels like sand – it could be gunpowder, for blasting in the quarry.'

'It can't be any good,' said Katie. 'It must be here since before the war.'

'I don't know if gunpowder goes bad, but this is as dry as

summer's dust. We could try a bit.'

'Bang!' said Katie hopefully.

'No, more like fizz I think, but not –'

Katie grabbed Dafydd's arm. 'Shhh. ... What was that? I thought I heard something.' They both listened. She could feel the pulse racing in Dafydd's arm. Then she heard the sound again, clearly, coming closer, paws on leaves, heavy crashing and panting. She wanted to get to the door to slam it shut but her legs wouldn't move. It was like one of her dreams, only worse. Then she saw it, bounding along their trail – black, baying. She gasped, and then gulped. It was not baying at all but whimpering. It was a real dog and it was lost. It looked at them in startled surprise. Dafydd said, 'Poor dog,' but Katie hushed him. 'But why, look, he's lost,' said Dafydd indignantly.

'Let him go,' whispered Katie. 'I know who he belongs to. I don't want this place to be found.' A sharp whistle rang out from the hill above. The dog's head shot up, and away it crashed in the direction of the sound. They waited till the noise had died away. Katie let go of Dafydd then.

'Gosh, that gave me a fright,' said Katie.

'I thought you liked dogs.'

'Not black ones.' She paused. 'Look, Dafydd, I should have told you before coming up here. You remember, last night, Seamus wouldn't say where they'd hidden the stuff they'd captured from the barracks in Nenagh?'

Dafydd nodded. 'Guns and ammunition, he said.'

'Yes. I've been trying to think where they might have hidden it. Remember, Seamus was their guide! Now, why did Seamus clam up when he came to that part of the story? I'm sure it was because the hiding place is somewhere near here. Then, just now there was a man in a trench coat talking to

Seamus down by the quarry, the same man that you heard talking up at Uncle Mal's. I saw him set off up here, and he had a black dog with him. I was sure then that this was where they'd hidden the stuff, but then the lock was rusted up, so the arms must be somewhere else. I wish I hadn't made so much noise.'

'So, it was nothing to do with the goats?'

'Look, Dafydd, I'm sorry, I should have said.' Katie felt suddenly ashamed. 'I know you want to be a quarry-man, I shouldn't have taken you away. We'll go back down now, I shouldn't have involved you.'

'I don't want to be a quarry-man, that's Dad's idea ... I want to be a reporter, or a mountain climber. I want to go back to school and become a genius, but that would disappoint Dad, wouldn't it? He's a slate man through and through,' Dafydd sighed. Katie looked puzzled and was about to say, but your Dad thinks it's you that's pushing to become a quarry-man, when Dafydd went on, 'What if you find the arms, or ammunition, or whatever? What then?'

'I'll tell Father about the guns, I suppose. He'll know what to do, but he's got other things on his mind at the moment. I just don't want him discovering them by accident, or anyone else getting to use them. And now there's this gunpowder. I don't want Seamus's crowd knowing about this either, God knows what they might use it for. I'd ... I just thought it would be fun to search together.'

'It would have been nice to have been told,' said Dafydd as he laced up his boots.

They had some trouble finding the lock where it had landed in the brambles. It was so rusty, however, that they were able to force it back into the closed position without it being obvious that it had been opened.

Another short, goat-sized tunnel led them out to the back of the tip again. Katie jumped a narrow ditch, climbed to the top of the tip and turned to look back up the hill over the trees where the magazine was hidden. Had the man gone up or down? she wondered. He seemed to have a way of disappearing. She waited for Dafydd who had stopped and was grubbing about in the ditch.

'Where are we?' he called.

Katie turned. She could see the last of the men leaving the quarry yard and disappearing down the hill, on their way into the quarry. There were no cables safe enough to carry a man now; they would enter through the cut. 'Directly above the quarry,' she said. 'Come on, they're gone down into the quarry now. Dad has opened the cave, let's go,' she said, jumping with impatience.

'Hey, don't jump or you'll start the whole thing sliding.'

'Ah, go on with you, the place is riddled with cracks. The goats are still in there, so we're all right. I'm going on.' She ran along the buckled railway tracks again, keeping well away from the frightening drop into the quarry below. Dafydd was scrambling urgently up towards her.

'Katie,' he called, 'you must come and look,' but Katie was not going back. She paused where a little iron hand-truck lay on its back, wheels in the air. 'Let's get down and see how Father's getting on,' she said. 'Come on, it will be quicker if we run down the fields.' She raced off, losing any reply of Dafydd's in the clatter of slates as she skated through the *sligins* to the field below.

CHAPTER 12

Traitor!

Katie crossed the road between the farm and the quarry yard where she had seen Paddy stop to mop his brow and went on downhill at a run, circling the tip heaps that spread like a skirt below the buildings of the quarry yard. Soon she could see where the tip parted to reveal the cut, an awesome crack in the side of the mountain and the only way into the quarry floor by foot. A small stream ran down it, and beside this was a footpath littered with blocks of slate that had fallen in from the walls above. Katie looked up apprehensively. A chill air met her and she remembered talk at home of men being killed while working in the quarry. She wondered with a shudder if their ghosts would mind this sudden intrusion on their peace.

As she emerged on to the quarry floor the towering walls appeared to be closing in on her. Opposite her was a black cave-like opening in the vertical quarry wall. She could see the last of the men disappearing into it now. Dafydd came up behind her.

'Come on,' she said. 'They've opened the cave, and I've never been inside. Years ago they tried mining the slate here underground.'

'Katie, don't go. I don't like it,' said Dafydd, pointing up. 'It's just under all that waste we were walking on ... and look there's a wet line all along the rock face ...'

But Katie wasn't listening. 'The cave has always been walled up before. Seamus and I tried to open a hole once to get into it but the stones were too heavy for us.'

'But it's not safe, Katie, I know about these things,' said Dafydd with sudden authority.

'Don't be silly, the men are all in there. Stay if you like.' She was beginning to be irritated by him.

Someone had left candle stubs on a slab outside, but there were no matches. She took a candle in any case and ducked in. Inside, the darkness was total. She groped forward, feeling along the walls until the passage opened out. There she stopped, hoping her eyes would adjust. To her surprise, Dafydd bumped into her.

'Might as well all die together,' he muttered.

At that moment a point of light appeared ahead as a match flared. Then the flame became two, then four, then more as the men grouped to light their candles from the next flame.

'Beautiful,' Katie heard Dafydd whisper. The gallery where the men were gathered was larger than she had expected. The points of light moved and wavered in the dark, sometimes showing up a face, sometimes glistening on the rock surface. Katie didn't want to go further. Somewhere just in front of her she sensed there was someone standing, like her also without a light – no point in asking him for a match. Then Father's voice broke the silence, magnified by the echo of the cavern.

'We are agreed then. It is good slate, but too expensive to mine underground like this. We are directly under the pile of waste we saw the children climbing a moment ago. All we have to do is push that waste down into the old quarry and start working from above. Once and for all, I vote that we clear the tip where we saw the children climbing just now and start again.'

'What?' Paddy Scully's voice rose in indignation. 'And you are asking these men to throw down from the hill all the waste we sweated blood to bring up the mountain! You must be mad, Eamonn O'Brien. You won't get any of my money for that, I can tell you. And, I'll tell you too, without my help you'll never teach the lads their skills – with or without a hook on your hand.' That was unkind! There was an indignant murmur.

Katie stared in fascination at the shift and movement among the points of light. Even as she watched, they showed as two clusters, one about Paddy and the other about her father. She could see Old Scully's face clearly – he had found a block of slate to stand on so the candles threw their light upwards, grotesquely, on his face. But the group about her father was growing. This was a sign, surely, that they were coming over to his side?

Suddenly, out of the darkness just in front of her, a voice barked out: 'Go back to England where you belong, O'Brien, and die for king and country if you wish.'

Katie lurched back against Dafydd, who steadied her.

'There's work to be done in Ireland before we start sweating for your profit and gain. We have a war to win. Now, lads, get out of here before it's too late and fight as you did against the English and against the 'Tans. Help us now to rid Ireland forever of the curse of English rule!'

The darkness moved in front of Katie. She put out a hand in a futile effort to stop the man, but he brushed past her while his voice still echoed in the darkness.

Pandemonium broke out. It was impossible to hear what was being said. The two clusters of candles broke up, amalgamated, and then began to stream towards the entrance. Katie turned and groped for the way out, guided by the blue glow of daylight. When she emerged she was dazzled but there was no sign of the man. She looked at her fingers. They still held the feel of his clothes as he had brushed past. He had been wearing a trench coat.

*   *   *

Father sat looking into his cup at tea-time as if it were a bottomless well. He took a deep breath.

'Fair dues to them, they came up, to a man, and said how he had no right to say those things about me, even old Paddy Scully, but it was like a wake or people shaking hands at a funeral. The quarry is dead, Mary. They said, "Just wait till the fighting is over," but I wonder. I'm tainted after the war, I carry an English smell. Anyway, they think there's too much work in moving that waste. We need a miracle, Griff, don't we? The whole bloody country needs a miracle.'

*   *   *

Evening. Katie had washed up and was in the yard throwing out the water when she realised that Father was gone. She went into the byre to where Peter was finishing milking, stripping the last drops from the teats.

'Where's Father?' she asked.

'Haven't seen him,' Peter said without looking up. Father wasn't in the house either, but she came on Dafydd, sitting on his bed, writing.

'What do you write in that copy-book?' she asked, but she didn't wait for an answer. 'Where's Father?' Dafydd didn't know. He put his book under his mattress and joined her in her search. She was suddenly very frightened – she didn't know why but she felt cramped in her chest. They found Mr Parry in the yard. She asked him if he'd seen Father.

'He said he wanted to see that the cave was walled up properly again,' Mr Parry said.

'I think I'll wander up and see how he's getting on,' Katie said tightly. Mr Parry looked at her. 'We'll come too,' he said.

There was nobody in the quarry yard, and the sheds were empty.

'Father!' she called. Mr Parry walked to the quarry edge and looked down. Katie steadied herself on one of the cables and leaned forward. All at once Father's voice came welling and booming up from the quarry below. Mr Parry grabbed Katie as she swayed. She couldn't make sense of what Father was saying. She looked at Mr Parry in dismay, but he was listening too. Then she realised Father was calling out names, names of people, name after name after name: 'Michael Feron – David Goodbody – Kevin O'Hanrahan – Sean Lyness ... ' at first the names were clear and loud, like a schoolmaster taking the roll-call in class, but then the echo in the quarry caught up with the names so that they overlapped one another in a continuous stream.

'What? What?' Katie found herself saying.

But Mr Parry was drawing her back from the edge. 'It's all right, Katie, I know those names.' He was trying to reassure her. 'It's all right, but I think you should go down. I'll tell you about it later.'

'To him you mean? Go down to Father?'

'Yes, can you face it?

'Why me?'

'Because I think you can help him, like you have in the past.'

Katie glanced at Dafydd – had he been giving her secrets away? But he was looking as dismayed as she.

She walked through the cut alone with her Father's voice booming louder and louder – magnified, distorted, urgent – still listing name after name and never once hesitating. The light was failing as she emerged but she could see that he had turned so that he could hear the echoes as they bounced back to him. She walked steadily towards him not daring to stop in case her courage failed.

He ceased shouting as suddenly as he had started. But the names lingered on, echoing and echoing, until eventually they faded into oblivion. She halted and they both listened. When she could hear nothing more she reached out for his hand.

'It's time we were going home, Father,' she said. He let her take his hand and lead him from the quarry. Tears were streaming down his face.

*   *   *

The lamp cast a pool of yellow light over the kitchen table. Mother had gone to help Father to bed.

'Whose were all those names?' Katie asked Mr Parry as she stood beside the range, her teeth still chattering with shock.

'Those, child, were the names of his friends, the men in his regiment killed in the war.'

'So many!' she said.

'Yes, so many.' Mr Parry paused. 'You know, Katie, that man who spoke out in the cave today, he got it wrong. We didn't go out to die for king and country, we went out as living ordinary people to try to make a better world for living ordinary people: you, our children, everyone.'

CHAPTER 13

Secrets in Welsh

Dad spoke to me in Welsh today. Worried like hell he is. He wants to know what she's told me about her Father, but it is washday and she is busy. I can't get near the house, let alone ask her what to say. Full of steam and women it is – terrifying.

* * *

It had rained in the night. Marty and Dafydd went off early on the creamery run with sacks over their heads like two monks. Katie went to fill the kettle with spring water from the bucket in the porch. When she came back Father was standing at the bottom of the stairs. She closed the lower part of the half-door, watching him as she did so. He was staring straight ahead. His eyes didn't follow her as she moved. It was as if he were blind! Katie stood still, kettle in hand, remembering when she was eleven and running down the platform at Nenagh with her arms out to greet him.

Huskily she said, 'Father?'

Slowly, very slowly, he began to thaw, his shoulders slackening. He rubbed at his neck. He smiled, but it seemed to hurt. Then he sat down at the table. Katie walked over to the range and lifted the kettle on to the hot-plate. She stood then with her back to him. Her future seemed to hover over her like a great black crow waiting to settle on her shoulders. She had it all to do all over again! Nursing, listening, cajoling, nursing, listening ... The pattern seemed to echo endlessly into the future.

She heard Mr Parry come downstairs, but she didn't turn to greet him. She remembered his concern last night, but she was hardening herself again. If she was going to nurse Father she'd do it on her own; she didn't need anyone else. All she needed was her own armour of misery.

They were still sitting over the remains of breakfast when they heard the wild clanging of empty milk churns as Marty turned the cart down the ramp from the road into the farmyard.

'We take it in turns with the neighbours to go to the cream-ery,' Mother explained to Mr Parry. 'Marty likes to go down during the holidays and get all the news. He sits there on a milk-churn with his cap on the back of his head and a straw in his mouth chatting about milk yields. I wonder how Dafydd got on? Wait now and we'll get the news off them.'

Katie filled the teapot from the kettle, then lifted the copper boiler on to a hot-plate and started filling it with rain-water. The water would have to be boiling when Breege arrived to help with the washing.

'I suppose you'll be thinking of going now, Griff?' said Father. His voice sounded tight and he swallowed as if there was something hard in his throat. Katie stopped pouring; it hadn't dawned on her that they might leave. Water splashed on to the hot-plate where it hopped and fizzled. 'It seems a shame to have dragged you all this way. I think we could have got Paddy Scully behind us if it hadn't been –'

Mr Parry cut in. 'If we could stay for another day or so, we'd like to. Dafydd says he wants to show me something he and Katie found up at the quarry and he'd be disappointed to go at once. Perhaps it's the secret of Paddy's magic goats?' he smiled.

'Oh! The blessed goats,' said Father absently. Katie crossed from the range and put her hands on his shoulders; the muscles were like bars of steel. He smiled up at her. 'Stay as long as you can, Griff, we'd miss you both if you went now, wouldn't we, Katie?' She looked across at Mr Parry and found herself suddenly wanting them to stay. She started massaging Father's neck and shoulders.

There was a scrape of boots at the door. 'Nobody will be going anywhere just now,' said Marty dramatically, 'the country is besieged.'

Mother froze, a sheet limp in her hand. 'Not invasion!' she gasped. 'Not the English ... they threatened ...'

'Not at all,' said Marty cheerfully. 'But all the roads to Nenagh are blocked with trees, and there are trenches dug across them too. There have been no trains since Saturday and they say the telegraph wire is cut. I think it's great, like a bad snowfall. Dafydd will be able to help me bring in the hay from the wet meadow now – it's beautifully dry, the rain was nothing. I'll make a farmer out of him yet.' Dafydd appeared behind Marty in the door.

'Bang goes your chance of posting your journal to Megan, Dafydd,' said Mr Parry, 'but keep on with it, this will soon be over.'

'Go and wash your hands, both of you,' said Mother, relieved. 'You can tell us all about it then.'

Katie, who had stopped, began to work her fingers into Father's neck and shoulders again. Marty returned in no time, drying his hands on his trousers and fishing in his pocket.

'Wait till you hear this. You know John Doran up at Knock? Well, in the middle of the night, John woke up. He had heard a noise in his yard, so, creeping out of bed he drew back the curtains, just a chink, to take a look.' Marty, the born actor, lowered his voice. 'There in the moonlight he could see someone moving about his hen-house. Now, John will tell you himself that he is a brave man, but the more he thought about it, and the more he took into consideration the times that are in it, the more his bed seemed a safe and comfortable place. Come morning he'd forgotten all about the incident in the night and went down to let the hens out. Horror! The door of the hen-house was swinging open and not a hen in sight. Inspecting the scene with caution he discovered, pinned to the door, a piece of paper on which was written this very message,' Marty held up a scrap of paper and read:

> 'Good morning John,
> Your fowl are gone,
> Your cocks will crow no more,
> You went to bed, you sleepy head,
> And forgot to close the door.'

'Is he raging?' asked Mother when they had stopped laughing.

'Divil a bit. He was just laughing at himself for a fool. He was showing the paper around himself, so I made a copy.'

'Perhaps it was in a good cause,' said Mother. 'Nevertheless, you'll take him down a couple of pullets next time you do the the creamery run. He's a decent soul and there's two hens about to lay.'

Marty had more to tell, but Mother was impatient to get the men out of the house. It was washday and Breege Connaughton, who came in to help each Monday, was edging in the door, trying to look invisible.

'Out, all of you, out now,' Mother commanded. 'Just because you're men doesn't mean you have to keep the chairs warm. Come on,' she cajoled, 'Marty, Dafydd too, snatch a slice of bread, the pair of you, and you can tell them the news outside.'

It was already raging hot in the kitchen. Katie was glad enough to have something to occupy her mind. The huge copper boiler that she had been filling was now steaming on the range. Upstairs the house looked like a swan's nest with blankets in heaps and the clean sheets folded on top, ready to be made up when the urgent task of washday was done below.

As the last of the men left, Breege became a different person. She lost her invisibility and burst into action, bossing both Mother and Katie as she tore into the weekly wash. They poured and carried, and steam billowed, and foam rose to Breege's elbows as she fished for items in the tub with a bleached stick and then worked them to the death, up and down, up and down, on the rippled surface of the washing board. Katie turned the handle of the mangle, watching the plump stream of wet cloth disappear, to emerge like a stiff board and crumple into the basket on the kitchen floor. Soon every bush in the garden was a mound of white and Katie thought her back would break.

'Look to the irons, Katie,' Breege ordered, and Katie took the heavy wedges of metal and arranged them on the hot-plate. In winter you could see the plate glowing red.

Breege dipped her head on to her shoulder to wipe away the sweat.

'Mary Mother of God,' she prayed, 'look on our souls and make them as white as our wash today.' She spat on the iron and noted how the spit hopped on the hot shiny surface. The oil-cloth had been taken off the kitchen table and the bare wood covered with an old blanket and then a sheet. Most of the brown stains on the sheet could be traced to Katie's experiments and moments of forgetfulness with the iron. For Breege, ironing, like everything else to do with the wash, was a steady flow of movement fuelled by tea.

'Would you wet the tea again, Katie dear. I'm parched with the drought and could soak up an other cup.' Katie had once counted the cups Breege drank, but Breege seldom actually stopped working. Just now she helped herself from the pot while Katie, using the fire tongs, drew out the cooling metal wedge from the back of the iron, slipped another blazing hot one in and slid closed the little door at the back of the iron. As she turned to the table with it, Breege's cup was down and her hand was out.

'I'll need the shirts next, Mrs O'Brien,' she called. Mother came in with an armful from the line and Breege spread the first of them on the table. 'It's a lonesome washing that there's not a man's shirt in,' she said and whammed the iron down. There was no man in Breege's house; she was an only child and her mother was a widow.

'You'd think,' Mother often said, 'with a fine stretch of land like that, some lad would have snapped Breege up years ago.' But Breege put all her energy into her washing. Without a flat-iron in her hand, as Father said, she became as invisible as the fairies.

By the time Katie got to sit down and Breege was tidying up, her head was swimming. The men began to appear, like hens at the door, taking a peek to see if it was safe to come in. The beds were made and the ceiling was hung with clothes and sheets airing. In winter they would have had to duck to avoid getting a slap from a wet sheet, but in summer everything was dried and folded.

'Doesn't it all smell nice and clean!' said Father. 'Breege, you've done us proud.'

But Breege was already invisible, pulling her coat over her sweat-stained dress. 'Good evening now, Ma'am,' she said as she sidled towards the door. '*Slán libh.*'

'*Slán agat*,' Mother replied, saying to Mr Parry after she had gone, 'there's not so many have Irish around here now, more's the pity, but Breege and her mother have it still.'

* * *

Dinner and tea became one on washdays, with cold meat from Sunday. It meant a nice long evening. Katie longed to get out of the house, which smelt oppressively of steam and Sunlight soap. Father and Marty went off to look at the wet meadow to see if it was hard enough to take the wheels of the hay float, Mother had gone to lie down, and Katie wasn't sure where the others were. She fed the chickens and stood in the door of the house undecided about what to do next. It was oppressively quiet. What now? Father's hopes of opening the quarry were gone. The elation she had felt after her talk with Dafydd had disappeared like the bubbles from stale lemonade. The black dogs were back, soon she would be on her own again; her talk with Dafydd had solved nothing. Father might be a hero but she had felt his muscles under her fingers and had seen his stare. Nothing had changed; just because Father had a medal didn't mean that he wasn't mad. Men in white coats could still come and take him away. The only comfort was that she had sworn Dafydd to secrecy. He was still the only other person who knew about Father's madness. Washday would come again and again and she would fade like Breege until she too became as invisible as a woodcock, to be brought to life just once a week in a sea of tea.

At that moment she heard voices approaching along the road. She strained her ears but couldn't catch what was being said. She had taken a step or two forward so she could see who it was when Dafydd and Mr Parry appeared, talking earnestly. They were speaking Welsh. Katie took a step back, feeling a sudden stab of suspicion. Talking Welsh was taboo according to Dafydd. She took another step back but was too late to dodge into the kitchen. They both saw her at the same time. No nod or wave of recognition; they just went on talking, looking in her direction. At that moment Katie knew, knew with absolute certainty, that they were talking about her. Dafydd had split on her. The chinks in her armour gaped. Her finger-nails bit into her palms. What were they saying? Mr Parry turned as if to retrace his steps towards the quarry and gave Dafydd a little push in her direction.

He had betrayed her. She waited, seething.

Dafydd walked carefully down the ramp into the yard. He was in bare feet. She felt a moment of scorn for a boy as old as herself who could not walk on stones. She turned, took off her apron and threw it into the kitchen, then she pulled the half-door closed to keep the hens out. She could feel her anger welling inside her. He had been talking! Let him come every painful step of the way.

He looked up from his passage across the cobbles. He had caught the sun over the last few days, or perhaps he was blushing. When he saw the look on Katie's face, however, he paled visibly.

'Dad asks ... would like ...' he stammered. Katie wanted to hit him but he was too big. 'Dad insisted ... he brought it up, I couldn't ...' She waited for him to go on, but he was stuck.

'Come on,' she said grimly and marched out of the yard after Mr Parry.

'I only ...' came his voice from behind.

Katie whipped around. 'Shut up, you streak – *shut up*!'

Mr Parry was sitting on the bank beside the road between the farm and the quarry where the view opened up in a broad sweep – to the meadows below, then to the village cresting the hill, and beyond it to the wide expanse of Lough Derg. As Katie

114

approached he got up, just as someone gets up for a visitor. He didn't smile but offered her a seat on the bank as if it were an armchair. She sat, and stared grimly out over the lake. He sat down beside her; Dafydd moved to sit on his far side. Katie was aware of her heart beating. When Mr Parry started speaking she could barely listen at first.

'There's a fine view from here; we can see uphill and downhill and each way along the road, and we will know if anyone is coming.' There was something in the way he spoke, as if she were grown-up and equal, that finally pushed Katie's indignation off balance.

'Katie, before you knock the head off my son here, there are two things you ought to know. The first is that I brought the subject up first, not him. The second is that we have only spoken about it in Welsh.' Katie stared ahead, so Dafydd *had* told him – and had told him about her silly game with the Welsh.

'It was a game,' she said sullenly.

'I'm not laughing at it, Katie. The world would be a better place if people learned the importance of games. Think what it means now. No words have been said here that anyone, other than us three, can understand. If you like, Dafydd and I will go away and never speak about it again. If you can let us in to share it with you, it will be just between us three and can stay that way. Your secret is safe.' Katie opened her mouth to speak, then closed it. She had been betrayed once, she needed to know more.

Mr Parry went on, 'I have seen your father in action in the war, Katie, and I can tell you that everything that Dafydd said about him is true. He is one of the bravest men I know, but his bravery is nothing compared to yours, especially as you were no more than a child when so much of it happened. I don't think you have any idea of how brave you have been. I take my hat off to you, Katie O'Brien, because without you your father would have been sitting staring at the wall in an asylum long since. Your father was far, far worse than I ever imagined. You haven't cured him, not yet, not completely, but you have to all intents and purposes saved his life.'

Katie felt she was in a bubble that surrounded her in a clear but tremulous film. She wanted to reach out to touch it but dared not in case it burst. The film was made of words, in Mr Parry's sing-song accent. Inside the bubble she was safe, Mr Parry and Dafydd were there beside her. How they had got in there she could not imagine. But now the bubble was expanding and expanding, freeing her in ever widening circles. The meadows below blurred as the meniscus passed, then the village swam briefly out of focus, the lake heaved and the film spread out, stretching to the horizon until it enclosed the whole world. She could feel the tears which had welled in her eyes moving down her cheeks. The pain of relief was almost unbearable. When Mr Parry put an arm around her shoulders it was all she could do to stop herself from turning and crying her heart out on his shoulder. This was the one thing she had resisted all these years – sharing – now she was lurching from pain to joy to pain.

Dafydd stared fixedly out over the lake.

'And now?' she managed to say, using her sleeve.

Mr Parry passed her a handkerchief. 'And now ... we have to move on, we must somehow make sure we don't lose it all.'

'All?' she asked.

He was slow to answer. 'Yes. All, Katie.'

CHAPTER 14

Father's Poppy

I didn't believe him, Megan, Dad that is – not till he told me about Will Morgan. You remember Will Morgan? Went barking mad in Bangor when he saw a dead horse on the road. Dad says that was shell-shock. With Will it was horses; loved horses Will did, and couldn't bear the way they were killed in the war. It took just this one dead horse to bring it all back. Will couldn't cope, see, he'd never talked about the war to anyone, then it was too late. Dad didn't mention Will Morgan to her of course, real gentle he was with her. I was proud of him.

* * *

Mr Parry had stopped speaking. They sat together on the bank, the three of them. Dafydd and Mr Parry spoke in low voices as the sun sank behind the mountains. For a moment the vanishing rim appeared to detach itself and hang like the segment of an orange above the crisp line of the hill. Then, with unexpected suddenness, it was gone. Katie picked up a twig off the road and started levering off the loose bark. She was only half-listening to their voices; they might have been speaking Welsh. They had told her about the depth of her father's shell-shock. In a way it came as no surprise. Deep down inside she had known, but what she hadn't known was how much she had needed friends, people like these to share it all with. For the first time that she could remember, she was not alone. What would she do when they were gone?

'So, what is it that sets him off, Katie?' Mr Parry asked. 'Is it words, like Seamus's outburst or the man who spoke out in the cave, or is it the fear of guns?'

Katie came back to the present with a jolt and old fears surfaced. For a moment the black dogs were ranging the hill behind her, then she pulled herself together. She saw Father's face again, pale and distorted, as he yelled at that piece of metal beside the road years ago.

'No!' she said, 'that's not it. It isn't the *fear* of guns that sets him off but *hatred*. He only has to see them to feel the hatred. Hatred of what guns do to people.' The stick she had been playing with snapped in her hand.

Mr Parry took her hands between his for a second. 'You know, child, I think you could be right. It hangs together, doesn't it? He had to stop that machine-gun before his men went over the top. I remember how he talked to them that night before the attack. He hated that gun because of what it would do to them. He often said he could never hate the Germans – it was the machinery of war that turned them into our enemies.' Mr Parry pulled a sprig of heather and began crumbling it in his palm, like someone rubbing tobacco for his pipe. Katie watched the pieces getting finer and finer. Eventually he held up his palm and blew the dust away. She noticed that his hand shook. 'You know, if it wasn't for the fighting here, he'd be all right. Probably never see a gun again. It's cruel – all he wanted from the war was to bring peace back with him. Did he ever tell you about the poppies in Flanders?' Katie nodded. 'We never could understand where they came from, but suddenly in spring, wherever the fighting had eased, sheets of red, red poppies would appear.' Katie remembered Father's description. 'Perhaps the seeds had been lying there for years waiting for this moment. Beauty and hope and life out of all that death. We used to collect the seeds from the little pepper canisters and scatter them far and wide. I remember your Father put some in a screw of paper one day. Said he would take them home to Ireland as Ireland needed a little hope too. Red poppies sown in a green field.'

'He must have lost them. We never found them in his things.'

'I think he found that he already had a poppy growing here.' Katie wondered what he meant but he did not elaborate. After a while Mr Parry asked, 'Your brother, Seamus, he's deeply involved, isn't he?'

It wasn't really a question but Katie nodded. 'Yes, and in a way, Mother is too.'

Mr Parry's next question caught her by surprise. 'Could you do without your father for a while, Katie?'

She jerked her head up. 'What ... what do you mean?'

'I mean you've nursed him for – what is it – five years. I know about it, Katie, he talks about you constantly. It's not just what I from got Dafydd here under torture.'

'To hospital ... to an asylum?' she whispered.

'Good God! No, child. No, no, no! With me and Dafydd to Wales. Do you think he'd come? We'd look after him. It's not just our being in the war together, it's chiefly the slate quarry. He could see how we do things in Wales.'

'I thought the quarry idea was dead.'

'Well, for the moment it is. It will take a lot of work to push all of that waste down and start again; there's no magic wand.' Dafydd made to say something, but seemed to think better of it. 'Really, the problem at the moment is that people here have other things on their minds, haven't they, with the fighting? Your Dad would be a born manager, I saw him in the war. His heart's not in the farming, not without his hand. Think of it, Katie, no guns, no Crossley Tenders. I promise we'd look after him.' The prospect seemed bleak but Mr Parry went on, 'Could you manage the farm between you if he came?'

'There's Peter. Marty would love it, and anyway it's holiday time. I'd help Mother, I suppose. It would be like it was in the war.'

'Seamus?'

'I don't know.'

'Perhaps he'd come back if your father was away.'

'Perhaps,' said Katie, but without conviction.

'Think about it, Katie. Dafydd and I will have to go once the trains are running again. Your father would be here, his quarry plans scuppered, nothing but Seamus to worry about, and the fighting to brood over.'

Katie knew she had no choice. 'Take him if he'll go,' she said.

'Good girl.'

By the time Katie was climbing the stairs to bed the first glow of relief was beginning to spread through her. Rather to her surprise she realised she would miss Dafydd when he'd gone. She did not hear Seamus return in the night.

CHAPTER 15

Haymaking

He had a gun – I'm sure of it – or I think I am. Something woke me.
There was a trickle of light from the little lamp they keep lit under the
holy picture. Gave me the creeps at first, that picture – all blood and
thorns. It wasn't Marty, but a man. I could hear him breathing. He
was just by Katie's door. What should I do if he went in? The
temptation to close my eyes and pretend I wasn't there was terrible.
Your Dafydd is not very brave at heart. Then the man seemed to change
his mind and turned towards me. It was when he turned that I'm sure
I saw the gun. It was Seamus, her brother. I had to close my eyes then
or they would have stood out like dinner plates in the dark. I wonder
should I tell her, Megan? Or has she enough to worry about?

* * *

Katie had volunteered to get breakfast but when she got
down the men were already tying their bootlaces in the
porch. Tying his own laces with one hand and his hook had
been one of the triumphs of Father's recovery. But Katie was
apprehensive.

'Morning, Katie, another beautiful morning,' called Father.
Katie's heart lurched. It was too loud, far too loud. She went to
the door and watched. Father seldom raised his voice, especially when people might be asleep. 'We're just going to block
up the entrance to the cut, far too dangerous in there. Must
keep people out. We'll need paint, Griff, for a sign.' Katie

wanted say Shhh! She even raised her hand as if to put a finger to her lips, but Mr Parry saw her and gave her a wink. The delicious feeling of being reassured spread through her. It reminded her of her soldier friend in Nenagh. She managed a weak smile and then listened to the scrunch of boots as they crossed the farmyard. Was it only a week since she had met Mr Parry and Dafydd at the station? She smiled, remembering her horror when she had seen Dafydd first. He was looking less sick now – with a bit of sun and feeding he was filling out visibly.

She put the porridge on and stirred, staring into the pot as she did so, remembering that trip to Nenagh. She thought about the soldier boy once more. Small chance of ever seeing him again.

Heavy steps on the stairs woke her from her day-dream. She turned, and Seamus was standing at the foot of the stairs easing on his jacket. She'd had no idea he was in the house – when had he come back? She hadn't seen him since ... when was it? ... Sunday, when he had been talking to the man in the trench coat. She could hear again that sarcastic, fanatic voice denouncing Father. She had actually touched the man as he passed her in the cave. She wiped her fingers on her apron at the memory. Seamus must have known the man was going to say those things! She could feel anger rising in her again like a blush. Who was it who had brought Trench Coat into their lives? Seamus. Who had started all this? Seamus and his blessed guns. Damn Seamus! she thought. Damn him! She turned back to the pot but the oatmeal was seething just as she was. She must think before she spoke.

Suddenly Seamus was behind her and was putting a firm arm about her shoulders.

'No "Good morning"?' he asked.

'Get off me!' she snapped, pushing him back.

'I just wanted to thank you for patching me up the other night,' he said, stepping back. 'There's no need to bite.'

'Bite!' spat Katie. 'Have you any idea, any inkling of what you have done? You, and that man in the trench coat, have destroyed Father's future, you've ruined his reputation, and you've brought back his shell-shock ...' She ran out of words.

Seamus shrugged and turned away. 'Grow up, Katie. Nothing was done on Sunday that wouldn't have happened anyway. Father's all right. I've never heard him so cheerful. He woke the whole house just now.'

'That's the point, Seamus!' said Katie in exasperation, letting a stream of porridge fall from her spoon on to the hot-plate where it hissed and bubbled. 'Anyway, what are you up to now?'

'Watch your spoon, Katie. Hush, here they come.' He added, in a lower voice, 'I want no more questions, understand?'

Katie blinked and stared at Seamus open-mouthed. Where had this sudden authority come from? Seamus had never shown authority over anyone.

Father was at the door, still talking with that booming artificial voice. As far as she knew, Seamus and he hadn't met since Seamus's outburst at dinner last week. What would happen now?

'We've been walling up the cut into the quarry, so nobody gets hurt in there ...' Father started. At that moment he caught sight of Seamus. Katie watched, holding her breath. For a moment Father seemed to be having difficulty in getting his eyes to focus, then he said loudly, 'Nice to see you, Seamus.' Had he really forgiven Seamus the things he had said that day at dinner? But Father was not acting normally. As if to confirm

123

this, he threw back his head, stretching out the tension in the muscles which stood out like ropes in his neck.

'Something burning, Katie?' said Mother. Katie started; the porridge she had spilled on the hot-plate had hardened and pungent smoke was streaming up. While she scraped at the crust with a knife she tried to listen to what Seamus was saying.

'I've asked some of the neighbours – and some friends – to help with drawing the hay up from the wet meadow, Father,' he announced. 'Barney will need a push up the hill as those cocks are always heavy. We'll make the stack in the quarry yard, as we did last year, it's a grand place.' Katie could feel the tension in the room. Mother had stopped in the middle of putting out the cups. The only person who didn't seem to notice the change in Seamus was Father.

'That's a grand idea. Some haymaking would do us all good. Yes, yes, let's move it then. I was down in the meadow with Marty only yesterday looking to see if it was dry enough. It will be good to get some use out of the quarry yard. Are you feeling strong, Griff?'

Katie looked at Seamus. Things were moving too fast for her. She'd always wanted him to stand up for himself, but now that he was doing it she wasn't sure she liked it.

'I'm game!' said Mr Parry, sidling up to Katie with a bowl for some porridge. 'I'll need some strength though, Katie, so slap it in for me!' Then he dropped his voice, 'I'm working on your father, Katie, he's nibbling. It's the idea of seeing a Welsh quarry working that's drawing him. We'll get him away all right in the end.' She opened her mouth to thank him but Seamus was talking again. 'It shouldn't be too hard, I have plenty of help lined up.'

'Marty will be upset if we do it without him – he's gone to get me some nails,' Father said. 'But help is not to be sniffed at. Let's make a day of it. Mother,' he called, as if she were in the yard rather than cutting bread at the small table, 'will you organise a kettle of tea for the helpers at twelve?'

'Of course I will, but I'll have to bake, we're out of bread.'

'I'll help,' said Katie, without much enthusiasm.

'No you won't. You look worn out after the washing yesterday, a spot of haymaking will do you good as well.'

*   *   *

Barney was already harnessed into the hay-float when Katie went out. It was a low flat cart like a huge pastry board on wheels. Peter sat on a sack with his feet over the front and drove, while Father sat on the opposite side. Katie, Dafydd, Seamus and Mr Parry rattled about on the back.

'Hold tight there!' called Father as the float tipped down the steep road.

'There's nothing to hold on to!' wailed Mr Parry. Katie watched, laughing, as he and Dafydd were gradually shaken closer and closer to the edge; in another moment they would be tipped on to the road.

'Hitch yourselves back up,' she laughed over the clatter of the iron wheels. 'Don't slide or you'll get splinters in your bottoms.' The road levelled out and Katie decided she might as well enjoy the day.

'That must be the most uncomfortable cart ever for riding on, I'm bruised blue.'

'Well, don't show us now, Griff,' said Father, laughing and pointing ahead. 'Will you look at the army Seamus has lined up for us.' The 'army' consisted of five men, Seamus's friends, presumably. Uncle Mal's Josie was the only one Katie knew by name.

'Hello, Josie,' she called as the cart swung in at the gate and the rattle of the wheels was suddenly hushed. 'Dropped anything?' Josie looked at his feet, then, remembering his dropped shotgun, looked up, grinned, and put his finger to his lips. They jumped to the ground as Peter backed the float towards the first cock.

'Back, Barney, back boy, whoah whoah.'

'That'll do,' said Seamus. The back of the float was almost resting against the cock.

Josie heaved on the lever which allowed the flat top of the float to tip up. The men pushed it down so that it formed a sloping ramp ready for the large haycock to be pulled up. Father was jumping up and down to test the softness of the field.

'It's fine and hard now,' he said.

Peter was looking at the haycock. 'What in the name of God have you been doing to this! Sliding down it like children?' he asked. The cock did look a bit ragged, but the men just laughed and crowded around, pulling out chains, unwinding them from the drums at the top of the ramp, talking among themselves and hooking the chains together at the back of the haycock. Then they came around to the front of the float and started working the levers back and forth, which tightened the chains around the cock. The oiled ratchets clicked and the haycock began to move. It was great having all these men. Seamus directed, but the men had all carted hay before.

'Isn't that a lovely sound?' Katie said to Dafydd, forgetting Seamus for a moment. 'The sound of summer and of carting hay.'

Slowly the haycock slid up the ramp until the moment came when the ramp tipped forward and, with a snap, became the flat top of the float again, only now the huge haycock was standing proudly on top. There was a cheer from the men.

'God above! Would you look at those wheels,' exclaimed

126

Peter, pointing. Even as they watched, the wheels were visibly sinking into the soft meadow.

'Come on, everyone,' Seamus urged, 'push. We'll be all right if we keep going. Either the field is wetter or that hay is damper than it looks.' Katie found a place at the side of the float and added her weight to the push. She avoided the circle of pale moist grass where the haycock had stood, as it usually crawled with slugs and beetles.

'Stay back of the wheel,' she warned as Dafydd thrust himself in to push in front of her. Barney strained, the men heaved and the cart lurched up on to the road.

'You'd all better come,' commanded Seamus. 'We'll need a push on the hill.'

'Please God they'll not all be as heavy as this,' said Father in wonderment. The meadow was almost directly below the quarry but the cart had to follow the road which circled round, then climbed the steep hill up to the farm and on to the quarry yard.

With so many helpers they took the hill at a rush. As they drove into the quarry yard Father said, 'A little help is worth a wagon-load of pity. That was great work.'

'We'll start by putting the cocks out by the quarry edge,' said Seamus, pointing to a place near the rim. 'We can build the stack over there then, close to the shed.'

'Go ahead,' said Father. 'Griff and I will put away the slates we had out yesterday.' Katie glanced towards Mr Parry who raised his eyebrows. Was this wise? A reminder of yesterday's failure – but in a short while she heard them both laughing. Well done, Mr Parry! If he could just keep Father on the laughing side of an attack everything would be all right.

Peter backed Barney up till they looked perilously close to the edge of the quarry.

'That'll do!' called Seamus from behind. The chains were undone and two of the men stood up on the back of the float to tip it up again.

'Take her away,' Seamus shouted. Barney lurched forward, as if he knew exactly what was needed from him, and the haycock slipped off the float.

'Like butter off a hot knife,' said Josie with satisfaction.

Katie, recalling the bumpy ride on the way down, called to Dafydd, 'Come on, take a twist of hay to sit on,' and pulled a hefty wisp out from the haycock.

'Hey!' came a shout from among the men. 'Leave that cock alone.' Katie turned in amazement. Whose hay was it anyway? Seamus snapped something at the men but she could not make out which one of them had spoken. Then one of them called out, 'Just a joke, Miss,' but it didn't feel like a joke to her.

'Come on,' she said to Dafydd. 'We'll walk straight down through the fields – it will be quicker. I'm not going on the float with that lot.'

They had reached the first gate when Seamus caught them up.

'What was all that about?' Katie asked, as they walked down. 'Which of them was it?'

'It doesn't matter,' said Seamus. 'The lads are all a bit edgy.'

So that's who they were, 'the lads'. Of course. But why would the lads take time off to cart hay for Father? She looked up at Seamus who was walking beside her, face set.

'Why are they here, Seamus?' she asked.

'No questions, Katie, remember?' he said. Katie bit back a tart reply. This was a different Seamus, he had to be handled differently.

'I want to talk about Father,' she said, but Seamus only increased his pace slightly. 'Seamus!' she challenged. 'He has shell-shock. He has it so badly that Mr Parry says if he gets another attack like the one you gave him last week he could be in an asylum for life.' She overtook her brother, turned, and backed down the hill in front of him. 'It's guns that set him off, Seamus. Guns! do you understand?' No response. 'What are you up to now? Why are these men helping us all of a sudden?' Seamus moved to one side. 'Don't you push past me! You're going to collect the guns from somewhere, aren't you, going to attack the barracks? Kill more people for Ireland?'

At that Seamus did stop and said between clenched teeth, 'Katie, this is a last warning. Nurse Father by all means, that can be your contribution to the war. My job is to fight it. There's nothing that a squeamish girl of fifteen can do – understand? Ireland is on the move again. Step back and let it pass.' Katie was damned if she would move, but neither could she think of anything to say. Seamus stepped round her and continued on downhill and Katie found herself looking up at Dafydd, who had been following discreetly behind. He gave an apologetic smile and a shrug. Obviously he had heard everything, but that was all right.

* * *

They had the second haycock up before Marty came back. When he did arrive Katie could see he was hopping mad that Seamus had come back ordering things about on the farm in his absence.

'What have they been doing with the cocks, Katie? It looks as if they've been gored by a bull.'

'Josie thought they'd been sliding down them.'

'Who are these men? They're not even local, apart from Josie ...'

'Friends of Seamus.'

'And what's turned Seamus into a farmer all of a sudden?'

Then he remembered something. 'Oh, Mother says she wants a hand to bring down the tea.'

'Is it twelve already!'

Katie decided to bring the food for the men down to the field. It was one pail of tea and another of sliced and buttered soda bread. Dafydd gave a hand. The soda bread was still hot when she took the tea towel off the top of the pail. The smell of it nearly killed her. She and Dafydd shared a slice for company, but 'family' would get theirs up at the farm when the next load went up – she wasn't carrying tea for everyone. Father, still laughing rather too loudly, told a story of how he and Mr Parry had been driven to the front in France during the war in a London bus with the old destination Camberwell Green still on the front. Josie managed a smile, but Seamus looked uncomfortable; the men just looked at each other and poked grass between their teeth. Katie remembered what the trench-coat man had said yesterday and wished Father would talk of something else.

Seamus's friends seemed to lose heart as the day wore on, and one after another they drifted away with a murmured apology, until only Josie remained. But the other haycocks were smaller and coming up easily, and soon the quarry yard was full of neat mounds of hay, ready to be piled into one large stack.

Katie, exhausted from the double walk, stayed in the meadow for the last trip, and Dafydd joined her there once he had helped push the float up the hill. She lay on her back and watched a lark soar higher and higher above them, singing and trilling, sprinkling her in a shower of liquid sound. She watched the fluttering speck until it turned, still singing, and flew down in great descending sweeps to the ground. It landed not far from Dafydd. She saw him freeze as the bird dipped into the grass in front of him. He walked slowly over to where it had landed. He wouldn't find the nest, not there – a lark always lands a little way away from its nest and then runs through the grass to it. But Dafydd stooped and picked something up. If it is an egg he'll keep it in his hand, she forecast, but he put it in his pocket. Some other treasure then, or else he'll have a messy pocket. She lay back again and let her arms and legs go limp.

'Look,' said Dafydd, standing over her.

'What is it?' Katie couldn't see against the light.

'Look!' He squatted down beside her. In the palm of his hand lay a row of bright copper cylinders, each narrowing to a silver point.

'What are they?' she asked, propping herself up on one elbow, but she instantly knew. 'Bullets!' she said.

'Live cartridges,' said Dafydd.

'Why are they stuck together?'

'They're in a clip, ready to load into the magazine of a rifle. You just press them in with your thumb.'

'Where did you get them?'

'Over there, where the first haycock was.'

Not lark's eggs then, she thought. 'But what are they doing in our field?' She realised that her mind was working slowly.

'Designed to kill,' said Dafydd darkly.

All at once Katie was wide awake. She sat up in one movement and turned to stare at where the first two haycocks had stood. How had she been so stupid? Seamus had fooled her, fooled all of them.

'Dafydd, I'm an eejit! An absolute and utter fool. That's ammunition, isn't it? That's what they took from Nenagh – not just guns but ammunition as well! Remember, Seamus said how heavy the boxes were? It was all here, hidden in those first two haycocks! We actually helped push it up the hill. That's why Seamus's so-called friends came to help us bring the hay up to the quarry – they knew it would be heavy. Remember what Seamus said about the boxes? Neighbourly love, my foot! First he ruins Father's hopes in the quarry, then he actually gets Father to push the arms he hates up the hill. What sort of monster is he? Remember how one of them shouted when I pulled a wisp out? This clip, as you call it, must have been dropped by one of them the night they hid it here. How could I have been so slow!'

'What if your Dad discovers it?' asked Dafydd.

'Father? God help me, Frog, I don't know. We've got to get him away, get him away now! I'll kill Seamus for this. Show me those things again.' Dafydd held out the shining clip of bullets on his palm like someone offering sugar to a horse. 'No,' said Katie, 'take them, show them to your Dad. He *must* do something to get Father away now. And I'll deal with Seamus, by God I will. That stuff will be gone out of here by tomorrow or I'm not Katie O'Brien.'

CHAPTER 16

Surprise Visitor

Katie had meant to climb straight up from the meadow, the way she had walked down with Seamus earlier, but in her hurry she had moved a bit too far to the right. She stopped, and looked upwards, panting. The quarry sheds loomed above her. To her right the black slice of the cut breached the grey tumbled wastes of slate. A freshly built wall closed off the entrance. Father had daubed large letters in red on the new-laid stone: Danger – Keep Out. Two trickles of paint ran down from the bottom of the K. Something black was lying on the ground at the foot of the wall; maybe Father had forgotten his coat there. She'd bring it in for him later. Hitching her skirt, she began to climb again. As she did so the black object moved. A head rose and she saw that it was a dog lying as if on guard. 'I know that dog,' she said to herself and pressed on harder.

A short last struggle brought her into the quarry yard, where she stood, breathless. There was no sign of Seamus and the yard looked deserted.

'Damn!' she muttered. 'He must have gone down with the float again.' She walked slowly between the haycocks. They stood like shaggy giants caught on the move, now standing frozen, wondering if they'd been seen. She walked forward cautiously. It was then she heard the voices. She stopped and listened, as one of the voices rose. It seemed to be reassuring the other.

'No, boy, the safest place for the sparrow is under the hawk's nest. Your father's reputation is our protection. The whole parish was here on Sunday and can vouch that there is nothing here. Your original idea was good.' Seamus's reply was low and she had to strain to listen. The one word she got was 'informer'.

'Don't worry, son,' then with a laugh, 'if you're not an informer yourself we'll be all right. I'll be off now.' Holding her breath she waited for the owners of the voices to appear. What were they up to? Then she swore: was there another way out? She ran forward and, as she did so, the door of the shed scraped open and Seamus came out alone.

She pushed past him into the shed, demanding, 'Who was that?'

'Come back!' he called.

But the shed was empty, just an echoing space. On the far side a shaft of dusty sunlight opened and closed across the floor as a loose sheet of timber in the wall swung backwards and forwards. Katie could hear the clatter of slipping slates outside then and knew she was too late. She turned and walked back out into the yard.

'How much did you hear?' demanded Seamus, grabbing her arm.

'Enough,' said Katie.

'Like what?'

'I know where the guns are, for a start.'

'We never mentioned that.'

'But I know, they're in the haycocks.'

'Katie, I warned you,' said Seamus, straightening himself up. 'You're under house arrest, and that's an order.' Katie's mind flew back to when they had been children together; this was ridiculous – but yet it wasn't ridiculous, he meant it. 'If you tell anyone about this or make the smallest move to interfere, or leave the farm I'll ...'

'Have me shot. That's what you mean, Seamus, isn't it?' said Katie, facing him down. For the first time that day Seamus looked uncomfortable, but Katie went on, 'Well, I won't make a move, Seamus, will I? Because that means telling Father, and whatever about you, I don't want to send Father to an asylum for life. That was really clever of you today, getting Father to help you push the guns he hates up the hill. You may even have been there when that man in the trench coat denounced Father in the cave, but you weren't there when Father started calling out the names of his friends killed in the war, were you? Oh no, you're never there to see the consequences of what you do. Listen to me now. Mr Parry is going to try to get Father away – you've got till then to move these guns.' She paused. 'After that I am going to destroy them if I can and you can have the pleasure of shooting your little sister.'

Seamus looked at Katie, and for a moment their eyes were locked together in equal combat. Did she see there a glimmer of respect? But she knew he could give as good as he got.

'Yes,' he said, then turned on his heel and walked back to the house.

*　*　*

'Throw that water outside, Dafydd dear,' said Mother. 'We never let water from washing our feet stand in the house in case it lets in harm. An old superstition really.' Tea was over and Father and Mr Parry were sitting behind empty eggshells.

Katie was drying her feet in the porch as Dafydd passed: 'Dad's winning,' he whispered.

Katie glanced into the kitchen.

'Mother, could you do without us for a couple of days?' Father asked.

'I'm sure I could. Young Dafydd here does more work than the pair of you together. But where would you go? Aren't the roads all closed?'

'Griff here wants to see the Broadford quarries while he has the chance. The weather's holding and a walk through the hills would do us both good. We worked him hard enough today.'

'When would you go?'

'First thing tomorrow. We'll stay the night with the Mac-Namaras.' He turned to Mr Parry, 'MacNamara's the one to swear that Broadford slates are better than Killaloe – they're not, but you'll like him.'

Dafydd joined Katie on the bench in the porch.

'Well done,' she said.

'It was the bullets that made him hurry it up, like you said. But what are *we* going to do?'

Katie smiled at the 'we' and stole a glance at the boy beside her. 'I don't know yet. Set the hay on fire, perhaps? Blow the whole lot up?'

'A bit dangerous, and it mightn't work. The hay was a bit damp.'

'I've got to do something but I'm not doing anything till Father's well away. I wonder if Seamus knows he's going?'

*   *   *

Morning dew drenched the grass when Katie and the two men left the track to climb the fields up on to the mountain. They were booted, but she was barefoot and swung her feet so that the wet grass ran between her toes. Father carried a stick and a satchel containing a substantial packet of sandwiches. Katie had also put in two bottles of stout and the corkscrew. She wanted to see them up the ridge on to the mountain – Tuontinna. She would have loved to have gone with them all the way, crossing the Shannon at Killaloe and then through the Clare hills to Broadford, but she had other things to do. She had lain awake last night planning where she could get her hands on paraffin and matches. She would have to act quickly because when Seamus heard that Father was away it would be a race between him and her.

Father stopped when they reached the top of the fields, level with the top of the quarry, and looked down. 'Good heavens!' he said. 'Seamus has already got the stack started. When did he do that?'

Katie looked down: the two haycocks from the quarry edge were gone and the base of a new haystack was laid out in a neat square beside the shed. Wisps of hay showed where the two remarkably large and heavy cocks with their secret store of guns and ammunition had been. So they were gone. It was at once a relief and a disappointment.

'It would be great if the boy took an interest in the farm,' Father was saying, then he turned to Katie, 'You turn back now, Katie. We'll be all right.' It was kindly meant, but the old hurt returned. The whole object of her staying at home was gone now and the feeling that he didn't need her returned. She looked at Mr Parry but he was anxious to get going. 'Come on, Eamonn,' he said. 'Just listen to that lark sing!'

She stood watching the men climb through the heather, and the whole mountain seemed to weigh on her shoulders.

*   *   *

It was afternoon and Katie rested, exhausted, on her bed, looking up at the ceiling. The sun was still high, striking steeply down on to the bedroom floor. It was so quiet she could hear the clock ticking in the kitchen below. They had all, particularly Seamus, worked hard that morning completing the haystack. She had not taken her eyes off him. The stack stood neat and square now in the quarry yard, and only one cock remained. For her part she knew that she could never in her life lift another hay-fork, let alone a wisp of hay. She examined her hands where two blisters rose out of reddened skin. She sniffed her hands; they smelled of paraffin. Dafydd had been poking around in the quarry yard during a break and had somehow got grease all over himself, but a paraffinny rag had taken care of the worst of it.

Nothing stirred so she closed her eyes again.

She must have drifted off for a moment because she was suddenly aware of the sound of voices below. Had there been a knock? Someone was talking – one of the neighbours probably. Her eyelids were beginning to droop when they sprang open again. There was something familiar about that voice. 'I met him a few days ago down in Nenagh,' the voice was saying. 'He said that there might be the chance of a job up here in the slate quarries.' In one convulsive movement Katie was out of bed and kneeling at the window. She missed Mother's reply and now held her breath waiting to hear his voice again.

'I'm sorry to hear that. So there's no chance of it opening now?'

'Not till the war is over, I'm afraid,' Mother said. 'People are thinking of other things. You're not from these parts then?'

'No, Ma'am, I'm from Galway.' Katie knew it! It was definitely her soldier. The accent, the voice were right. She remembered now that, as they had driven out of the station yard, Father had said something about handing in his rifle and teaching him to split slates. The voice went on, 'I was in the army till a few days ago, but my six months are up. I heard there was the chance of a job up here and thought I'd give it a try.'

'Well, I'm sorry about the job now, I hope you haven't lost out all round.'

'Leaving the army you mean? No, Ma'am, I'm glad to be out of it. I didn't know which side to be on. Friends in both.'

'Won't you stay and have a cup of tea? It's a long way from Nenagh.' Katie gripped the window ledge. Would he even recognise her if she went down? She heard another window open in the house but didn't give it a thought.

'I won't thanks, Ma'am. I got one last perk out of the army – a lift in a barge to Garrykennedy. There's a contingent landed there, came by lake as the roads are closed. I have most of my walking in front of me.'

'Mother of God!' said Mother. 'What's the army wanting around here?'

'They're not telling, but there was a load of arms and ammunition taken in Nenagh last week. They'll be after that, I'd say. I think they have a tip-off.'

'Oh really?' said Mother. Katie could sense that she was

138

anxious. 'So you'll cross the Shannon at Killaloe, and then go up to Galway through Clare?'

'If you could just point me the way.'

Katie glanced desperately down at herself. She wasn't even dressed, and she daren't move away from the window – she just had to hear.

'Of course I will,' said Mother, stepping out into the yard to point. 'Follow the track below the quarry and up through the gap in the hill; look, you can see it. You'll find some old standing stones there – we call it the Graves of the Leinstermen. Follow your nose downhill and left into Ballina, then cross the bridge into Killaloe. Come back again when the trouble is over.'

'I will indeed, Ma'am. Good day.'

Even from above, Katie could recognise him as he crossed the yard. She had to do something! She couldn't call out, she wasn't dressed properly, and in a moment he'd be gone from her life for ever. It was then that she saw Dafydd sitting by the shed with his copy book. He looked up and smiled at the young man as he passed. Katie waved frantically, but Dafydd didn't notice. He looked down at his book again. She tapped at the window and nearly screamed as he looked everywhere but up at her. Then he did look. She pointed at the receding figure and put a finger to her lips urging him to follow. For an agonising moment Dafydd didn't seem to want to understand. 'Go after him,' she mouthed. 'Stop him!' Dafydd dropped his eyes and appeared to lose interest in her. Then, just as she was looking for something to throw at him, he closed his book, slipped it into the front of the cart, and set off after the man.

'Bless you, Frog ... I love you ...' muttered Katie grudgingly as she pulled her dress over her head and frantically buttoned up the front. She tore her fingers through her hair and glanced

139

in the mirror. She looked wild, but what matter! She pulled open the door of her room and there, facing her on the landing, was Seamus. They stood staring at each other. He was in the act of pressing a clip of cartridges into the magazine of a rifle.

CHAPTER 17

Dafydd's Plan

Katie stood transfixed. Seamus pressed the last round down into the magazine, flicked the empty clip from the breach with his thumb so that it bounced away and lodged against the end of Dafydd's bed, then he slid the bolt forward and moved the safety-catch to 'on' with a snap. Was it for the boy outside? Her soldier? 'Squeeze the trigger,' the voice in her dream had said, and Seamus and the boy became connected now in her mind in one violent percussion and one violent death.

'Stop!' she whispered. 'Seamus, please stop,' but Seamus's eyes were not focussed on her, it was as if he was staring at some horizon she couldn't see.

'You don't understand,' he said, 'it's got to be done.'

What had to be done?

'Don't hurt him, *please*,' she whispered.

'Who?'

'The boy who was here. You were listening from your window.'

'He'll be all right if he goes away. If he doesn't he's probably a spy.'

140

Yes, and Katie knew what they did to spies. 'What will you do?'

'I've got work to do. It seems the Free State army is on the way.'

'Will there be fighting?'

'You heard. It could be an opportunity. It depends on what the informer knows.' Seamus's voice softened for a moment, 'I'm glad Father's out of it.'

'Isn't there another way?' she asked.

'I've got to go.' The moment of softness had passed; he was looking through her again.

* * *

She saw him go down the stairs, slipping his arm through the sling on his rifle as he went. She waited till she heard his footsteps in the yard and followed him down. Mother was standing at the kitchen table staring at the empty door. Katie wanted to stop and reassure her, but there didn't seem to be anything reassuring to say. She made a small, helpless gesture with her arms and slipped out too.

She climbed the steep slope out of the farmyard and turned right towards the quarry, and to her surprise Seamus was ahead of her. She'd presumed he'd go left and follow the road up to Uncle Mal's, the way she had taken Dafydd on that first day. Had he decided to hunt the young soldier after all? To her relief then she saw him climb the fence and head off up the hill. Of course – over the hill – that would be the quickest way to Uncle Mal's. Dafydd and the boy were standing in the road together, both staring after him. She started to walk towards them. She had day-dreamed about this moment ever since her trip into Nenagh, but now that it was actually happening she wanted to run away.

The boy had taken off his jacket and had slung it over a

canvas bag which hung from his shoulder. His shirt had no collar, but it was clean and open at the neck. He looked sunburned and fit. Only his cropped hair showed him for a soldier.

Katie looked down shyly as she approached. She could think of nothing to say. Her mind had gone blank, panic was rising in her and, to her dismay, she heard her own voice saying, 'You looked better in your uniform.' She glanced up, aghast. It wasn't even true – why had she said the very opposite to what she meant? But for some reason he looked pleased.

'I thought you looked like a Maeve,' he said with satisfaction.

'Maeve?'

'You reminded me of Queen Maeve in her chariot when I saw you at Nenagh. Your speech of welcome fits. But perhaps you don't remember mere stable lads.'

'Oh but I do, and you were nice to Barney.'

'Poor Barney, he didn't like that train. But it's strange what you say about my uniform because, from what I am seeing now,' and he looked up to where Seamus was just climbing out of the fields on to the heather, 'a Free State soldier in or out of uniform might not be too popular around here.'

'Are you still a Free State soldier?'

'A spy you mean?'

Katie blushed, annoyed with Seamus for having put the thought into her mind, but the boy smiled. 'No – I've left the army,' adding, as if that needed some explanation, 'it may seem silly, but I never thought, when I signed on for six months, that I might actually be expected to kill people.'

'Yes ... I mean no,' said Katie – it didn't seem silly at all. She looked up to where Seamus was just climbing out of sight. 'I don't think he's thought about it either. You men are just dreamers.'

'Is that the Fiery Cross running up the hill?'

'The Fiery Cross?'

'Yes, that's how the Scots raised the clans. A burning cross was carried from clan to clan. It raised more than mere dreams in the past.'

'I think it is.'

'You didn't send him then?'

'No, he's burning on his own.'

'So, what is your command, Maeve? You're not really a Maeve, are you?'

'No, I'm Katie — Katie O'Brien. But please, we've got to stop them.'

'Stop them? Or stop him? You're not being clear, Miss O'Brien. I haven't got wings, or a gun for that matter. Who do we have to stop?'

'We've got to stop them all, on both sides,' said Katie, running her hands through her hair, knowing it sounded silly.

'All I did was to come up looking for a humble job in a slate quarry, and now I'm being asked to stop a war. Perhaps you weren't listening, Miss O'Brien, but I'm running *away* from war. I'm not the stuff that warriors are made of. You must learn to recognise a coward when you see one. Cowards don't stop wars.'

'Oh but they do – and I bet I know more about so-called cowards than you. Stop playing games – call me Katie – tell me your name, and help me think.'

'My name is Kieran and I'm an expert in helping Katies to think.'

'You say the army has a tip-off that the arms taken at Nenagh last week are here.'

'Yes,' he said.

'Where are they now?'

'The arms?'

'No, the soldiers,' said Katie.

'They're making their way up here, I imagine. I saw them start – spreading out and searching barns and out-houses on the way. Anywhere arms might be hidden, looking busy just to satisfy the sergeant, and hoping they won't find anything. The officer's all right, but the sergeant's nasty, really nasty.'

'But will they look up here?' she queried.

'Certainly. The quarries were mentioned – they have information.'

'Well, they're too late. The guns were here but they've gone.'

Dafydd, silent till now, began to say something, but Katie cut him off. He'd been standing a little to one side, looking dark and morose. He'd never looked morose before, and it made her uneasy.

'Leave it, Frog,' she said. 'Kieran and I have got to get this straight now because things are going to start happening soon.' Dafydd turned on his heel as if he was about to go off, but she added hastily, 'Don't go, Dafydd, please, it's just I ... I must just explain it all to Kieran here.'

Dafydd sat down on the bank, rested his chin on his hands, and glared at the road while Katie told Kieran how the arms had been brought to the farm by Seamus, why Father must never know, and how she had wanted to set the haycocks on fire.

'I wanted to get rid of them, you see, and destroy them utterly so they couldn't hurt anybody ever again!' she declared. But I'm all confused now,' she explained. 'The guns have gone and Seamus is spoiling for a fight and I don't know what to do.'

'I–' began Dafydd.

But Katie's mind had darted off. 'We could send them on a wild goose chase,' she interrupted.

'Explain,' said Kieran.

'I could go to your officer and say the guns had been moved to Killaloe, or ... or somewhere.'

But Kieran shook his head. 'They'd suspect a trick. They'd never trust anyone from here.'

'But they'd believe *you*!' she said with sudden inspiration.

'Thank you! And who'd be shot when they found out, you heartless girl? And if they don't get the guns who will? Your brave Seamus? Is that the idea?'

'Oh dear, it's impossible, isn't it?'

'*May I –*' snapped Dafydd.

They both jumped.

'I think your brother wants to say something,' said Kieran unnecessarily.

Dafydd took a deep breath. 'Thank you,' he said, clambering to his feet, a formidable shamble of arms and legs, as he turned to Kieran. 'Brother, my foot! Dafydd Parry, from Wales, and nobody's humble servant. If you and that gabbling girl are capable of listening to sense and reason I will tell you where the guns are.'

They both stared at him open-mouthed.

'Where?' they asked in unison.

'Why didn't you say?' added Katie unwisely.

Dafydd swung on her. 'Because no – one – would – listen to me!' he said between clenched teeth. 'Come on, come with me.' Without waiting for an answer he set off at a run in the direction of the quarry.

*   *   *

'Don't touch that cable, it's got grease on it,' warned Dafydd as they hovered cautiously at the quarry's edge among the wisps of hay remaining from the haycocks, peering down into the dark chasm below.

145

'So, that's where you got all that grease from last night,' said Katie, scanning the quarry floor. 'Well, where are they? I can't see anything, can you, Kieran?'

'Just a hole,' he said, shading his eyes.

'But they *are* there,' said Dafydd.

'They can't be, Dafydd. There's only one way of getting into the quarry and Father's walled it up. Come on, Kieran, I'll show you.' She ran at a safe distance from the quarry edge, past the new hay-stack and the old sheds, to where the quarry yard was cut off by a vertical gorge which ran from the quarry out to the hillside below. 'There, that's the cut, there's a path and a stream down there.'

Kieran leaned forward. 'It's a horrible place, all right,' he said, 'but why couldn't they bring the arms through there?'

'I said, because Father has walled it up.'

'But walls can be taken down and rebuilt.'

'Yes, but not this one. Father has painted 'Danger – Keep Out,' all over it. You'd never rebuild it without it showing.'

'And it hasn't been disturbed?'

'No, that's why Dafydd's story doesn't make sense ...' Katie looked at Dafydd. 'Why are you grinning?' she asked.

'The cut may be the only way in, but it's not the only way *down*,' said Dafydd.

'Go on,' said Kieran.

'Some of the older quarries in Wales still use cables, like this one here – lots of them spanning the quarry. You have a special double pulley: one wheel runs on the cable, the other wheel takes a rope or cable which goes right down to the quarry floor. The men load the slate into a bucket so it can be hauled up and then pulled into the quarry yard here.'

'So it would be quite easy, if you had a pulley and plenty of rope, to reverse the process and lower ammunition boxes or guns down on to the quarry floor?' said Kieran. 'What then?'

Katie's mind, which had become tangled with the talk of pulleys, now jumped ahead, 'Oh Frog, clever Frog! The cave.' She grabbed Kieran by the arm and pointed. 'Look, down there is a place where a hole has been walled up. That's an old mine in there, it's like a cave.' She hesitated. 'But how will we know? I'm not swinging down there in any bucket.'

'I doubt if they'll have taken the rope with them – and there's the pulley as well, that would give a clue,' said Kieran. 'Anyway, they'll want the stuff out again, won't they? What's in those sheds?'

They searched urgently among the dust and the debris left by the old slate workers, stepping over the sprouting remains of seed potatoes which had been stored there last year. As a last resort Kieran pulled some boards forward, and there was the rope, bright and new, still smelling of fresh hemp. The pulley, just as Dafydd had described it, was old but well greased. Katie fingered the rope.

'I still wouldn't like to be lowered down on that,' she said. 'The men must have climbed in some other way, and that has to be down by the cut. 'If they can, we can. How much time do we have before the army gets here, Kieran?'

'I don't know. I can't think why they're not here now!'

'Come on.' Katie led the race out of the quarry, circling the skirt of waste slate below to where she had seen Trench Coat's dog the day before. There was the end of the cut and the wall which Father had built still blocking it. His scrawled warning was clear and undisturbed.

Dafydd scanned the rock beside the wall. 'Look,' he said in triumph. 'Nail marks, like you see where they've been climbing in Wales. Men have climbed the rock here.' With the agility of a spider he scaled the rock. 'Put your feet where the scratches are,' he instructed as Katie climbed.

'Well, they didn't bring ammunition boxes up here,' she gasped, taking his out-stretched hand.

A sloping shelf of rock made the descent into the cut easy. She ran down in front of the others, jumping fallen boulders, and out on to the quarry floor. Here she stopped. The floor of the quarry was bare rock and broken slate. No point in looking for scratches or footprints here. Wisps of hay lay scattered on the ground from the haymaking above.

'I hate this place,' said Dafydd looking up unhappily. 'Anyone seen the goats? Perhaps they've emigrated?'

'What do we do now?' asked Kieran, peering at the wall which now sealed off the cave. 'Are the guns here or are they not? That wall looks solid.'

Katie stared at the wall as if, by looking hard enough, she could see through it. Pieces of hay were stuck between the blocks, and idly she pulled one out. 'This wall is saying something to me and I can't make out what it is. I suppose we'll have to make a hole.' She stared at the wisp of hay in her hand. Then she whipped around. 'Stop, everybody, I've got it! Hay! Frog, you're a genius. Look, there's hay caught between the blocks. On Sunday, when they closed this up, there was no hay anywhere near here. They took the wall down and built it up again last night. The guns are in there, sure as hell. Now we've *got* to open it!'

'We'll never have time to take it down stone by stone,' said Kieran. 'I'll look for something that will do as a crowbar.'

'Well, be quick. Remember the army's coming,' said Katie, heaving at one of the great blocks which formed the lower part of the wall. It seemed immovable, but at the same time she thought she felt a slight tremor in the wall as a whole. 'Dafydd,' she said. 'Come here and feel this!' She heaved again. Yes! It was infinitesimal, but the wall did move. Whoever had built it, had built it free-standing, probably just so it could be pulled down quickly. Katie was not going to reason why. Together they both threw themselves at it.

'Get the rhythm, Katie,' Dafydd commanded as the wall began to rock. The next push would do it.

'Now!' It was going ... going! But, too late Katie realised one end had stuck. Instead of falling in it was going to fall out on top of them. 'Watch out!' she yelled, leaping back, trying to pull Dafydd with her. With a snaking movement half of the wall came forward, while the other half fell back. It split in the middle and the two halves crumbled and rumbled to the ground. Katie fell, wondering if this was how it was to die. Then she felt herself being lifted back as Kieran pulled her clear. 'Dafydd!' she called, struggling to her feet, 'is Dafydd out?' But Kieran turned her, laughing, to where Dafydd stood dazed, unscathed, and grinning. Katie darted over and gave him a hug of relief, only to back off, laughing and choking in the dust she had raised.

'Look what we've done!' she said proudly.

'You two are crazy!' said Kieran.

'It just started rocking, and then it sort of tumbled out rather than in. We were lucky.'

'You're each as bad as the other,' said Kieran resignedly. 'Now what?'

'We look inside. I wonder if there are any of those candle-ends left?' Katie approached the entrance with care, but the wall had fallen clean away from the living rock. Sure enough, there were half a dozen candle-ends scattered just inside the entrance. She picked one up. 'I bet we haven't any matches.'

'Hold on a minute,' said Kieran, one hand deep in his jacket pocket. 'There's something in the lining here that feels like a match.'

'Is it a red-head? Otherwise we won't be able to strike it.'

'Red-head it is!' he said triumphantly, blowing the fluff off a single match.

'Come inside,' said Katie, 'we can't afford to have it blow out.'

The match struck easily on a piece of slate, and they advanced cautiously into the cavern, each with a lighted candle.

'I can't see anything,' said Katie, searching. 'Surely we got it right? The stuff must be here.'

'Yes, it is! Look!' Dafydd's voice came from behind them. They turned. At first Katie could see nothing. Then the candle-light caught something that seemed to weave and flow. Her stomach tightened. It looked just like a snake, glistening, and moving as she moved.

'Careful, Dafydd! Snake!'

He jumped back. 'But there aren't any snakes in Ireland!' he protested. 'That's not a snake ... but what is it?'

Kieran moved forward. 'It's a belt of cartridges for a machine-gun.' He reached for the end. 'The belt feeds in at the side of the gun. It fires the bullets out at hundreds a minute.' So they had found the cache!

They examined the pile of weapons in awe. The machine-gun was there, and a number of rifles like the one Seamus had held. But the important part, according to Kieran, was a neat stack of wooden boxes with numbers stencilled on the sides and lids.

'What does 303 mean?' Katie asked, trying to lift one of the boxes.

'It's ammunition; point three-o-three gives the size of the bullets.'

'Gosh, they're heavy. We'd never move this lot even if we could find somewhere to hide it. Oh please, somebody, tell me what we can do! I hate this place and I hate what's in it.'

* * *

Some minutes later they were standing outside the cave. Katie threw the stub of her candle angrily into the black entrance.

'I won't give up!'

'Look, girl, stop arguing, and Dafydd, don't you start! This is not a case of an old musket or pike thrust into the thatch. These guns, especially the machine-gun and the ammunition, are worth a fortune to the side that gets them.' Kieran was getting angry and his voice was rising.

'That's what I *mean*!' said Katie.

'But this is *serious*, Katie. Those men are going to come in here fighting, there will be blood and war here at any moment. I've got to get you out.'

'Thank you – I'll look after myself. Listen, I heard Father calling out name after name after name in this very quarry. The names of all his friends killed in the war. That was serious too, Kieran!'

Katie paused for a moment. 'It was his roll-call of the dead. I *won't* give up! I can't. Not while those guns remain.'

'But, child,' said Kieran putting an arm round her, 'there is nothing, absolutely nothing we can do!' She threw his arm off.

A pigeon, which had been resting on the slate tip above their heads took off with a clap of wings and flew off down towards the valley. A chip of slate no bigger than a shilling pattered and bounced down the face to land between them. Dafydd stooped and picked it up.

'But there is,' he said. 'There *is* something we can do.' Dafydd looked almost as stunned as they did when he said this.

'Go on,' said Kieran.

'I've been thinking about the goats.'

'Goats?' echoed Katie in a daze.

'Let him talk,' said Kieran.

'It's like this, see. The reason our dads don't want the men working down here is because of the danger of the *sligins* – or whatever you call them here – waste slate anyway, falling into the quarry on top of them. Like this chip, only bigger. I've been thinking, if enough waste were to fall down into the quarry it would cover up the cave, guns and all.'

'But only little bits fall, Dafydd, and only after heavy rain. It's as dry as a bone now and Father said it would take months to shovel it all down,' said Katie, disappointed.

'Which brings me to the goats,' said Dafydd doggedly. 'When Katie took me up there on Sunday it was to see the goats, or that's what she said. Well, I saw the king of the goats, all right, but I also saw not just one but several cracks in the ground at the back of the waste tip. It looked to me as if the whole tip was going to slip into the quarry then and there.'

'Was that what you were poking at?' said Katie. 'You should have said.'

'I did say, several times but ...'

'Now, hold it, you two! But is there any way to make it slip, Dafydd, short of high-explosive?' asked Kieran.

'Yes, that's it. I think there may be.'

'God above!' exclaimed Katie, hand over mouth. 'The magazine – the gunpowder we found. I wonder if it's any good?'

'It's good all right. I tried a pinch – it flared up beautifully,' said Dafydd with a grin.

'Come on,' Katie called. 'The sun's going down and we're just standing here.'

CHAPTER 18

Counting Elephants

Why had they left it so late? The vertical walls of the cleft blurred as Katie raced towards the entrance. She could see a wedge of sky above the wall at the end; two cottonwool clouds drifting across it were glowing pink. The sun was setting already. She ran up the ledge that led out of the cleft and was about to show herself above the wall when Kieran said, 'Keep down, Katie! Look first.' She raised her head cautiously, half-expecting to see an army lined up below with glittering trumpets, flags and pennants. But the fields and hedges stretched out innocently towards the lake. The only moving thing was a man bent into the hill, climbing fast towards her. He turned like a fox viewing its trail, and she froze, expecting hounds to break out of the hedges below, but the hedges kept their secret. Kieran joined her.

'Look!' she whispered. They lowered their heads instinctively as the man began to climb towards them again. His walk was fast but furtive. Katie shivered – that was how the black dogs in her dreams moved. The scene became chill and menacing. They waited until the man veered to one side and disappeared around the edge of the tip. 'He's going straight over the hill,' she said.

'That man looked hunted,' said Kieran. 'You saw how he turned? We'd better get moving. Look, we can climb straight up the waste to the sheds above, can't we?'

The climb up the loose slates was far harder than they expected and they reached the top gasping for breath. Poor Dafydd, still weak from his illness, trailed behind, so Kieran waited for him which meant that Katie stepped into the quarry yard alone. A voice rasped out behind her: 'Hey! Hey, you there!'

She spun around and then froze. She was looking down the barrel of a short, stubby, wicked-looking pistol. The man who was holding it was standing a few yards off, breathing heavily. So he hadn't climbed straight on up the hill, she thought.

'You O'Brien?' he asked. 'Seamus O'Brien's little sister?' Katie's tongue seemed glued in her mouth, and she nodded. 'Now, listen to me. I've got no time to call at the farm,' he continued. 'You're to give Seamus a message, and God help you if you don't.' She swallowed. 'Tell him the Staters are coming. Got that? They know we have the stuff – he'll know what I mean by that. But they're not sure where it's hidden.' Katie nodded. 'We have to make them think that the stuff is up here in these sheds.' Katie thought of the gaping hole in the quarry below, just behind the man, and forced herself not to look in that direction. 'We'll wait till dark, then we're going to pretend we're moving the stuff. That's what they'll expect us to do so we'll go along with that. We'll show lights moving here as if there are men working in the yard. Seamus is to organise the lights.'

'Won't that just bring them on?' asked Katie, gathering courage.

'Precisely. That's the whole idea. We ambush them here.'

'Oh, I see,' she stuttered, then added, 'Good,' and hoped it sounded convincing. The man seemed relieved and thrust the pistol back into his pocket.

'Now repeat the message,' he commanded.

Katie repeated it.

'Good. When he's got the lights ready he's to come to the meeting place.' At this the man looked up the mountain. 'What's the quickest way over from here?'

Instantly Katie realised he mustn't go near the quarry edge. She pointed quickly to the nearest route away from the edge and then watched with beating heart as he skirted the quarry before disappearing up the hill.

'He's gone,' she called, heaving a sigh. The boys emerged cautiously. 'Fat lot of good you two are, leaving me staring down the barrel of a pistol while you skulk behind a haystack,' she laughed, hoping to cover the fact that she was shaking.

'You were brilliant!' said Dafydd.

'Of course I was!'

'Thanks to you we know their plans,' said Kieran. 'We also know how much time we have – a little over an hour perhaps. Can we do it in that time, Dafydd?'

'Let's go,' Dafydd said. 'I've never tried anything like this before.'

*   *   *

'Oh stop dithering, Frog! Bash the lock off with a stone like we did last time. Can't we just throw a match in the door and run? The light is going and –'

'Shut up, Katie! We'd be blown to bits. Anyway we're too far from the cracks to start a slide,' said Dafydd. 'Take your boots off, Kieran.'

'Ah for God's sake, Frog, we've no time for that!'

'Do you want this to work or don't you?' snapped Dafydd, straightening up and glaring at Katie. Katie was silenced. 'I wish I'd thought about all this earlier,' he said as he hunted around in the shed. 'We've nothing to carry the powder in.'

'What about your cap?' Kieran suggested. But that was no

good. It only held a little and when they carried it to the crack the powder just trickled down into darkness below.

'It must be held together, packed tight!' Dafydd complained, squatting back on his haunches.

Katie was panicking now, trying to keep her mind on the subject, but every rustle or flutter of birds or animals in the grass had her twisting and turning. She thought of paint tins from the farm, but they'd get jammed in the crack ... there was nothing in the harness room ... then she had it – *socks*!

*   *   *

She emerged from Seamus's room, having riffled his drawers to find Dafydd scribbling hurriedly in his exercise book.

Megan,
In case I never come back, bury me in my boots, my feet aren't hard enough for hell yet. You won't find any socks. Now I must go.

'Good heavens, Dafydd, you're not writing your journal now!'

Dafydd shoved his exercise book hurriedly under his mattress with a grin. 'I was waiting for you. The last will and testament of Dafydd Parry. Moving, isn't it?'

'I weep for him.'

'Have you got the socks?' he asked.

'Yes. Why didn't I think of this before – no more darning.'

'We need a hurricane lamp.'

'In the kitchen.'

'And I have matches. Where's your Mother?'

'She's up with Mrs Moran, usually goes on a Wednesday.'

*   *   *

'You were long enough!' Kieran whispered when they struggled up from the field on to the tip to where he was keeping watch. The sunset was no more than a blush in the west.

156

'Dafydd had to write his will.'

'Seen anything?' Dafydd asked Kieran.

'Nothing and everything. A blackbird has alarmed twice from below, and sheep have been moving down from the hill. Both sides closing in, I'm sure of it. But I just hope they wait till it's completely dark. We haven't a second to lose.'

*   *   *

Desperately they began to fill the socks with black powder and lay them out like sausages on the floor. Dafydd used a small wooden scoop which Kieran had found. 'They'd have used this to load the charges in the old days,' he informed them. It was hot in the enclosed hut and sweat ran down their faces. They lit the hurricane lamp which Dafydd placed outside the dusty window on the quarry side of the magazine.

'Woops! This one has a hole in it,' exclaimed Katie. Their hands were black and their faces were streaked where they had wiped them. 'We're getting powder everywhere. Nobody breathe fire! What do they make gunpowder out of, anyway?'

'Charcoal, I think,' said Kieran, 'and something called saltpetre.'

'Of course, you'd know about it from the army,' said Katie.

'They don't use gunpowder now, they use other explosives. Gunpowder made too much smoke. Couldn't see the enemy after the first volley.'

'Not even the whites of their eyes,' said Katie. 'Well, let's hope this stuff will go off. There's quite a lot left but that's the last of the socks.'

Dafydd was outside, crouched over one of Father's blue handknitted socks. Katie winced. She remembered Mother knitting those.

'Do be quick, Dafydd. What's the rope for?' she asked.

'Not rope,' he mumbled, 'fuse. I tried it while you were

doing the washing, before Dad got me. It burns at five elephants a foot.'

'Elephants?'

He took out the cartridge which he had been holding in his mouth like a cigar. 'One elephant, two elephants, three elephants,' he said. 'It's a way of counting seconds.'

'I wonder how many elephants before we have an army on top of us?'

'Are you using that cartridge as a detonator to make sure the powder explodes?' asked Kieran. Dafydd nodded as he wound the fuse around the shiny cylinder, thrust it inside the last sock and tied it off with twine. 'Where did you learn all this?' Kieran added.

'He works in the slate quarries in the holidays,' Katie explained.

'I've never seen the final loading up though,' Dafydd complained. 'They always send me away before the detonators go in. I hope this works.'

'I hope so too,' said Katie. 'I'll be murdered over the socks whatever happens. Come on! We'll all be murdered if we stay here. Ready?'

As quickly as they dared they carried the bulging socks over to the crack and packed them in, side by side, wriggling them deep down to where the tip had started to detach itself from the mountain. A curlew called from the hill, a haunting call. Using the wooden scoop until it broke, and then their hands, they covered the charge, first with earth and sand and then with larger and larger blocks of slate until, instead of a crack, there was a grave-like mound. Only the snaking fuse showed where the charge had been placed. The light had gone and it was now quite dark.

'Shhh ...' whispered Katie. 'There!' A whistle came from

up on the mountain. It was answered by another away to their left.

'Light that fuse!' Katie commanded, but the boys were arguing.

'Look you, whose idea was it? Anyway, you don't know how to count the time.'

'All right,' said Kieran. 'But you must make sure you know which direction to run.'

'Never run,' said Dafydd, but he came with them as they descended the hill to rehearse his escape route once the fuse had been lit: up on to the tip, along the old railway line, past the little up-turned truck, and then down into the field. He turned back at the truck.

'Good luck!' They listened to the click of slates as he disappeared into the night. Katie started calculating the time. He would be on top of the tip now. She shivered. Kieran put an arm around her shoulders but she hardly noticed.

'He'll be at the fuse now,' she whispered. The slate tip stood in front of them, a black bulk rising against the fading sky. 'He'll be taking out his matches.' She put a hand on Kieran's; she could feel his tightening on her shoulder. Forty elephants, Dafydd had said. He had plenty of time.

Katie started counting. A late lamb bleated in the fields below. There was a smell of bruised grass. 'Four elephants, five elephants, six ...'

They saw the flash long before the sound hit them. It lit the sky and burned the scene before them into their eyes: the outline of the tip, a stunted thorn tree, stark fence posts. The bang that followed was ear-splitting and vicious. Katie could feel a scream rising from deep inside her.

'Frog!' she yelled, lunging forward. Kieran tried to hold her but she broke free and he lost his balance and fell.

'Come back!' he called, but she was already struggling up the tip.

'Frog,' she sobbed as she reached the top. There was the up-turned truck. Bushes seemed to be on fire somewhere ahead, but her eyes had been burned out by the flash. She found the railway track and started along it. At that moment Dafydd hit her, head down, knocking the breath out of her and sending her flying. They fell in a tangle of skirt, arms and legs.

'Go back,' he yelled. 'It hasn't gone off yet. I was knocked down. I've forgotten my elephants.'

'Are you all right?' she gasped, holding him, while he struggled.

'Yes – the magazine blew up, I don't know why. But our charges haven't –'

This time there was no flash. It was as if the whole mountain had woken with a belch from a drunken sleep. A growl like thunder rose from the ground as the entire tip seemed to rise under them.

'Run!' yelled Dafydd, pulling Katie up. 'Oh Lord – which way?' They were both in bare feet. Something strange was happening beneath them. It was as if they were standing on liquid and the stones were flowing under a thin skin.

'This way!' they heard a voice calling, and there was Kieran in the flicker from the burning bushes. They ran. He grabbed them and half-pulled and half-carried them down the slope. They hit the flat of the field with a jolt and found themselves sprawling on firm, gentle grass. They turned to look at the tip.

Above them the outline of the tip was changing. The stunted thorn tree, lit now by the glow of the fire, was gliding down the slope. Then for a dizzy moment the little railway truck appeared on the sky-line, on its wheels for one last crazy trip before it careered out of sight down into the quarry below.

The whole profile of the hill was changing in front of their eyes; where there had been a mound there was now a gentle slope.

The low thunder of the fall died away to be replaced by the lighter sound of slipping slates.

'It's gone,' whispered Dafydd. They sat in silence while the enormity of what they had done sank in. Katie groped for Dafydd, found him, and hugged and kissed him, meaning it as a 'thank you, thank you for so much – for listening to me when I opened my heart to you down at the lake – for betraying me to your father – for having faith in me when I wanted to destroy the guns.' She wanted to say something, anything!

'You did it, Frog, you did it!' It seemed silly and melodramatic. 'And I thought ...' but now she was crying. 'Sorry, Frog, ... I'm just so glad you're all right.'

'It will take a lot of digging to get anything out from under that pile,' said Kieran.

For a long while Katie and Dafydd sat clasped together listening to the crackle of the burning bushes and the singing in their ears. Katie wanted to go on holding him, loving him as he deserved to be loved, but she could sense that he was uncomfortable.

'Maybe we should get washed up,' he said. 'I suppose we can be expecting visitors.' He struggled, and Katie, reluctantly, let him go. 'Funny,' he said, 'I'm still counting elephants.'

She watched as his small figure disappeared into the gloom. It had all happened so quickly. She realised she was seeing Dafydd for the first time for his true worth, but she also knew that she was losing him. She struggled to her feet, watching the familiar figure disappear. Kieran was standing back as if he understood what she was feeling.

'I love you, Frog,' she called out into the night. But there was no answer. Downhill, in the distance, men were shouting.

She groped behind her and found Kieran's hand. She pulled it over her shoulder and held on to it.

'I think we should get away from here,' he said. 'You've done it, Katie. You've done what you set out to do, haven't you?'

'Not me, Kieran. Not me,' she said, and pressed his hand against her cheek.

CHAPTER 19

A Miracle from God!

Dafydd had a lamp lit by the time they reached the house. The yellow wedge of light looked welcoming and homely. Katie poked her head into the kitchen, leaving Kieran outside.

'Anyone else here?' she whispered from the door. Prince circled her legs, whining his welcome.

'No, there wasn't even a light. I wonder where Marty and your mother are?' It seemed strange to Katie that life might be going on as it always had.

'Oh, I remember now, Marty was going to help Mr Moran with a calf. Mother will have waited for him there,' she said. Dafydd came to the door, holding the lamp. Katie gasped and then laughed. 'Have you seen yourself? You look like a chimney-sweep!'

'In that case, Miss O'Brien, you look like the goose that was dropped down the chimney to clean it.'

'Water is what we need, lots of it.' She stepped outside to signal to Kieran that the coast was clear, then stopped to listen.

There were shouts from the direction of the quarry then the rapid 'crump crump crump' of nailed boots pounding in step towards them. 'Inside, quick!' Katie ordered, then there was a command from the road. 'Now lads, up the hill, and we'll have them.' Boots scraped, men cursed and crashed as they pushed their way through the hedge, then there was silence.

'Dafydd and I'll wash in the trough,' said Kieran.

'No you won't, you'll come inside.'

'They're gone now. You go in and wash, we'll get the worst off out here.'

*　　*　　*

Katie sat on the end of her bed. The boys had joined her now and were working hard with soap and hot water to get the last of the black off their faces and necks. They made quite a contrast in size and shape.

'I can't believe it, I just can't take it in,' she said, hugging her knees. 'We did it! We really did! Here's a towel.' She threw it to them and they fought over it amicably. 'All those tons and tons of rock like a river in flood. Wasn't it strange the way it turned to jelly under our feet – then the roar, and the little railway truck! Oh, Dafydd and Kieran, just think of all that lovely rock on top of the guns and nobody knows how it got there.'

'Well, we hope they don't,' said Kieran. 'What did you do, Dafydd? Did you mean to blow up the whole magazine?'

'No. I didn't set it off, I couldn't have,' said Dafydd. 'But it knocked me out for a moment. I seem to remember ...' He paused. 'I was just about to light the fuse and I heard a sound from up at the magazine. I was petrified. Was there somebody there? Or was it the goats, perhaps? My hands were shaking so much I was afraid I wouldn't be able to light the match. What if someone saw me when I struck the light? I decided I'd shout a warning, but only when the fuse was alight. The head broke off my first match and I nearly dropped the box. When the second match flared it seemed to light up the whole mountain. Perhaps someone had me in his gun-sights now, but the wretched fuse wouldn't light! Then all at once it started, spitting and hissing all over the place and burning awfully quickly. I looked up but staring at the match seemed to have blinded me. I had to get out – and I had to start counting my elephants. It didn't seem possible to shout and count at the same time. I must have been looking in the direction of the magazine at that moment because I'm sure I saw someone strike a match. Almost immediately there was a blinding flash, a huge bang, and a thump that seemed to hit all over me, and everything went black.' Dafydd began to scrub at his hair with the towel.

'Go on,' said Katie breathlessly.

'Well, next thing I knew I was struggling to my feet and scared silly. There was something terribly wrong, you see. My mind was saying: twenty elephants, twenty-one elephants ... Either I had lost count in the blackness or else I had just nineteen seconds to get away. They say never, never run from a blast. By God I ran.'

'I know, you hit me going at full tilt.'

'Funny feeling wasn't it?'

'No it wasn't, it was like being hit by a cannon ball with legs,' said Katie.

'No, I mean when our explosion went off – like a big burp it was, and the whole mountain lifted and you were holding on to me like I was a thief. Then Kieran was calling and we knew which way to go.'

'So your elephants were right.'

'I reckon I was one elephant short, must have been counting them in my sleep. Kind of exciting, wasn't it?'

Kieran looked at Dafydd who had started working away at his hair again. 'Dafydd, you're amazing!' and then he began to laugh. It started as a chuckle, and Katie could see it coming and was already smiling when it burst. She tried to keep a straight face but Dafydd's half-serious, half-puzzled expression was so comical she had to laugh too. Through her tears she saw Dafydd grin and then give up the struggle. All the tension, all the anxiety, all their fears went romping out around the room as they collapsed in hysterical laughter.

After a time Katie's laughter began to subside in painful hiccups and a fervent wish that no-one should start her off again. She cocked her head and put up a hand for silence. Light, running steps could be heard outside and Mother's voice calling, 'Children, children, are you all right?'

Katie took a deep breath. 'Yes, Mother, we're fine,' she called down.

'What happened?'

'It sounded like an explosion up towards the quarry.'

'What on earth can have caused that?' Mother sounded worried.

'There are soldiers up there.' Katie had her fingers crossed for the next question but a man's voice was calling from the road, 'Missus, excuse me, Ma'am. We're looking for a young lad who we think may be around here. Well built, tweed jacket and a ... what sort of a pack did he have, Sergeant?' Katie looked towards Kieran, who made a face. A second voice answered; it had an edge to it that Katie didn't like. 'Sort of satchel. We think he may have been involved ...'

'All right, Sergeant. We'd just like to talk to him, Ma'am.'

To Katie's relief Mother answered without hesitation, 'Yes indeed, he was here. That would be the young lad who called – when – when was it – just after dinner. He wanted a job in the slate quarry. I had to send him away, I'm afraid. There won't be work here till after the war is over.'

'Which way did he go?'

'Oh, along past the quarry. I sent him up through the gap to the Graves of the Leinstermen and down to Killaloe. He'll be in Clare by now.'

'Oh well, that tidies that up, thank you, Ma'am.'

'What happened?' Mother asked.

'There's been a band of rebels operating out of these parts. We think one of them blew himself up. Bomb-making probably.'

It hadn't occurred to Katie that someone might have been hurt. A sudden fear struck her and she gripped Kieran's arm – Seamus? He knew about the magazine. The voice went on, 'We found this.'

Now Katie *had* to see. Kieran tried to stop her but she darted to the window, edging forward so she could look down without being seen. Two men in uniform were lit in the wedge of light from the door. She saw the glint of a polished Sam Brown belt and a bandaged hand on the man in front. She drew back, remembering the fallen tree and a long-barrelled revolver. The man behind passed something forward that looked like a sack. The officer held it out.

'What is it?' Mother asked.

'It's a trench coat, Ma'am. Anybody you know wear a trench coat?'

'No. I've never seen it.' Katie could sense the relief in Mother's voice. 'Is there a ... a body?' Mother asked.

'No, Ma'am, no body, just this in the bushes. If there was a body his friends took him away.'

'Or he was blown to bits,' said the other voice.

'Thank you, Sergeant!' snapped the officer. Then, talking

to Mother, he tipped his head towards the quarry. 'Is that your land there, Ma'am?'

'Yes, oh yes, the quarry too. My husband hopes to open it again.'

'Well, he'll have his work cut out, I'm afraid. The blast the owner of this coat set off started a regular landslide. The quarry's half-filled up again from what we can see.'

'Oh ...' said Mother vaguely, but the soldiers were ready to go.

'We'll take that, Ma'am, if you don't mind. It's evidence.' Mother handed back the coat. 'That'll be all. Thank you, Ma'am. Better keep inside till all this is over.' The officer turned and walked away. The Sergeant hesitated till the officer was out of hearing then said to Mother, 'We'll be back.'

Katie shivered. She waited till the scrunch of their boots had receded into the distance, then whispered, 'You heard that?'

Kieran nodded. 'There are some in the army that learned more from the Black and Tans than is good for them,' he said.

'He meant it then?'

'He either meant it or he enjoys scaring people. It works, you know, scaring people at random until one of them does something silly.' Katie gazed at her two friends, both looking scrubbed and anxious. She loved them both. She wanted to see Father's face when he came home and found all his work in the quarry done for him and the new rock laid bare. She wanted to tell him how they had buried the guns. Mother would prepare a special dinner for him and for Mr Parry, and Katie'd stand up and say, Look at my clever boys! She closed her eyes and the fantasy faded.

'You'll have to go, Kieran, it's dangerous for you here,' she said.

'I don't think it's me he's after now. I don't like to leave you with him around.'

'Who is he after – Seamus?'

'Could be ... else he just likes making trouble, like I said.'

'You still ought to go.'

'I can't, not while you're all in danger here.'

'Yes you must, really and truly. We'll be all right, and there's nothing you can do. In fact, if you were found here it would just make things worse. Whoever they were they would presume you were on the other side and want to shoot you. If they realised you'd buried their toys under thousands and thousands of tons of slate they'd probably join together for the fun of tearing you apart.'

'Maybe you're right, I don't want to make it worse for you.'

'Of course I'm right, amn't I always right? Dafydd will tell you. We'll hide you in the loft above the harness room till the soldiers have gone. The only trouble now is that Mother's in the kitchen. I'll have to go with you to show you the way.' She turned to Dafydd. 'Frog, can you think of a way to get Mother out of the kitchen, just for a minute, while we dash through?'

*   *   *

Katie hovered half-way down the stairs, one ear cocked to hear what Dafydd was saying and one hand held up ready to signal to Kieran when the coast was clear. She could hear Dafydd's voice below. Why did he sound as if he was complaining? What was he asking?

'Perhaps there's a pair in the wash I could wear?' came his voice as he led Mother towards the pantry where clothes for washing were kept.

Stifling a laugh, Katie signalled urgently to Kieran above. He slipped swiftly down the stairs, boots in hand. They raced across the yard, hand in hand, and darted in behind the saddle-room door.

'Did you hear him, Kieran?'

'No, but it sounded as if he was complaining.'

'He was. He was telling Mother, as if it was her fault, that he had been looking for his socks everywhere but he couldn't find a single pair!'

Katie could feel one of Kieran's deep chuckles rising in him, she pressed him to her to squeeze down the chuckles and wanted to put a hand over his mouth to stop another outburst of laughter.

'Complaining about his socks! You won't find another like our Dafydd,' he chortled.

'You'll find a ladder at the back of the room,' Katie said finally. 'You'll be safe up there. I'll bring you out some food as soon as I can get to the larder, but you'll have to wait till Mother goes to bed.' She ran back across the yard.

*   *   *

Mother wanted to hear all about the explosion, but there wasn't much they could tell. Just how there had been a loud bang followed by a roar, which they supposed was the rock-fall the soldier had mentioned. Katie's fingers were cramped from keeping them crossed behind her back in case, but lies weren't really necessary. Nevertheless, Mother was restless. She wanted to stay up for Marty, but Katie assured her it could be hours yet and that Marty'd be all right if she left a lamp lit for him. Still Mother lingered doing odd jobs. In the end, in desperation, Katie went up and got ready for bed herself. At last she heard the door of Mother's room close. She took a breath of relief and made her way to the larder to engage in honest theft.

*   *   *

Katie stood outside the harness room with Kieran's satchel in her hand and her pulse racing. Little fears flitted across her mind like bats. She felt strangely vulnerable in her nightdress under the stars but he wouldn't see her, it would be dark in the loft.

She climbed the ladder to be met by impenetrable blackness.

'Here, Kieran, take your satchel. It has some scraps in it.' She heard him move. He must have felt the satchel because it was pulled away from her into the dark.

'Gosh! you didn't have to kill the pig for me!' his voice said appreciatively.

'Just some old scraps that Prince refused,' she managed to say as she pulled herself up on the opposite side of the hatch to where he sat. It was just like the time they had first met in Nenagh. Words just would not come. Her tongue felt like a great blob in her mouth. She felt shy and awkward. There were still sounds of activity on the hill outside, occasional shouts, a shot. It seemed natural to keep quiet. Eventually a squad of marching feet passed and a deeper silence settled over the farm. She tried to see where Kieran was in the dark. She forced her tongue to move: 'Have you got the food I gave you? I don't know how you'll get the cork out of the bottle.'

'Don't you worry, I haven't been a soldier for nothing.' It came as a surprise to hear his voice and to know that he was smiling. For a moment her confidence flooded back.

'You'll come back for your shirt, won't you? I'll wash it and keep it for you.' She'd borrowed one of Father's old shirts for him to wear and had taken his powder-blackened shirt to wash, but really it was as a keepsake, something of his to hide in a drawer till he would come back.

But time was running out. Barney shifted in the stable next door. In the distance someone was whistling. That would be Marty, keeping his courage up on the dark night. Perhaps

Kieran was just waiting for the chance to get away from this crazy girl and her divided family. Just keep talking, she told herself. 'You know how to go?' she whispered. 'Don't go near the quarry, not the way Mother told you. Keep straight uphill along the townland boundary. It'll take you straight up the ridge. Follow the ridge to your right then, over the top of the mountain. There's a little lake up there. Then drop down into the valley and keep on downhill into Ballina, avoiding the lake-side. If they're really looking for you you'll be across the bridge and into Clare before they get there.'

Why was he so silent, she wondered. What was he thinking? She could hear him breathing.

The whistling was close now. Marty, for sure. The calving must have gone well.

'I must go, Kieran, that's Marty whistling, I'll have to slip in with him.' With a huge effort she got up. The trap-door from the loft showed as a dim rectangle. As she stepped on to the ladder her nightdress caught on a nail. Still he was silent. As she lowered her head and began to free herself she was close to tears. Suddenly there was a movement in the darkness in front of her. She raised her head in surprise. Kieran's hands were holding her lightly but firmly by the shoulders and she could feel the warmth of his breath on her face.

'You crazy, lovely girl,' he said. She looked up and suddenly their lips were together. Time stood still for Katie then. Later, over the bleak time that followed, it sometimes felt to Katie as if that kiss had only lasted a second, at other times it seemed to have lasted a week. Certainly it would have gone on forever if her nightdress had not torn itself free and she had not half-slipped, half-tumbled down the ladder.

'All right?' came an anxious whisper from above.

'Yes! I love you, Kieran, come back please,' she whispered.

Marty was washing himself in the trough as she flitted across the yard and in through the darkened porch. Mother had left a lamp burning low for him on the kitchen table. Katie had a foot on the stairs when Marty came in.

'Well! What's this? *More* trouble?' he asked, grinning. Katie put a finger to her lips. Mother's voice called down the stairs, 'That you, Marty? Put the lamp out, dear, will you?'

'A little Hereford heifer, Mother, a real beauty,' Marty called, blowing out the lamp with a wink at Katie.

* * *

The day that followed passed in a daze of tiredness and anticlimax. There was plenty to do because Mother had planned a special dinner to welcome the men back. It was just like that fateful day nearly a week ago when Seamus brought the war into the house with his sudden outburst at dinner. He was at home this morning looking drawn, tired, and nervous, glancing forever towards the door or watching the road from the cover of the porch. A steady trickle of people passed, going up to peer into the quarry and to wonder at the fall of rock. Many of them would have heard the explosion but none of them called at the house.

'Why don't any of them come down?' Katie asked Seamus after a group had passed without a glance into the yard.

'They don't know where we stand,' he muttered as he drew back from the door. 'Nobody trusts anybody now.'

Katie wanted to talk to Dafydd – perhaps together they could capture again something of the wonder and triumph they had all felt last night. But Dafydd seemed to be avoiding her.

Marty was full of excitement at what had happened the previous night.

'You should go up, Katie,' he said. 'It's amazing. From the quarry rim right up to the start of the bushes there is just one sheet of shiny rock. It's as smooth as a baby's bottom.'

'Marty!' exclaimed Mother, laughing.

'But it is, Mother. Even I can see it's good slate too. Then down in the quarry there's this huge pile of *sligins* spilling right over the quarry floor. We'd never have moved all that by hand.'

Eventually Katie made the excuse of going to meet Father and Mr Parry. She wound her way up to the quarry and stood gazing down into the hole in awe. It was quiet now except for the occasional forgotten slate which slipped down the slope and tinkled into the abyss. A noise from one of the sheds caught her attention and she found Dafydd there, poking among the old tools and equipment.

'Dafydd! I never really thanked you. It's quite a sight isn't it?'

'It's that all right.'

'I ... I just wanted to say thank you,' Katie tried again, but Dafydd seemed more interested in his poking. She got the feeling he didn't really want to talk. 'It is good, isn't it? The slate on the hill?'

'Can't really say till you get into it, but it looks good.'

'I can't wait till Father sees it, and your Dad of course.'

'Can't you?'

What was wrong with him? This was a big moment and he was moping. Katie could hear Father's voice and see the two men in the distance now. Instead of being glad, Dafydd seemed chilled. Suddenly the conversation they'd had up by the magazine flashed into her mind. What had he said? 'I want to be a reporter or a mountain climber or,' and Katie had to smile, 'go back to school and become a genius.' So that was it! Here was Dafydd, who had dared to blow half Tipperary into the sky, dreading to meet his father, and all because of a silly misunderstanding.

He was making for the door literally dragging his feet. This was ridiculous! Katie leapt over a fallen box and ran to cut Dafydd off. She turned and seized him by the shoulders. He seemed to have grown since his arrival. She fought to hold his eyes as she stumbled out her explanation. 'You pair of eejits, both. Your Dad wants you to go back to school, whatever about becoming a genius. He just thinks you are set on becoming a quarry man. Wake up, Dafydd Parry, Wales is waiting for you!' As she spoke she saw his eyes widen in doubting comprehension.

'Go on, go out there and ask him,' she challenged, and stood back.

She let him go and watched, fingers crossed, as he walked over to the two men who were now staring down into the half-filled pit. She saw Dafydd and Mr Parry turn to face each other like two images in a mirror, then she imagined that she saw Dafydd draw a deep breath. She held hers. Suddenly Mr Parry threw back his head and laughed out loud, stepped back, scratched his head and laughed again.

Dafydd turned towards Katie with a grin and a shrug, as if to say: What can you do with a dad like that?

*　　*　　*

Father was standing alone, looking up first at the bare mountainside, then gazing down into the pit below, oblivious to them all. Katie came up beside him, still smiling to herself, and put an arm about his waist.

'And they tell me no-one was lost in the blast,' he said, shaking his head. 'It must have been the old magazine up there in the bushes. Katie dear, it's a miracle – it's a miracle from God.'

CHAPTER 20

The Search

'I think you should go,' argued Mother. 'The quarry will keep, and this isn't the time to be starting it up again. What time did the man with the boat say?'

Father was polishing his hook on his trousers. 'I just don't like leaving you alone with all this army activity.'

'I'm not alone. Seamus says he'll be at home now, and we have Peter and Marty, and it's the holidays. Go on, tell me, what was the arrangement?'

'When we were talking to McGrath in Ballina he was saying he would take his barge up to Portumna, possibly even to Athlone if the wind is right. They're running out of wheat for bread in Nenagh, with the roads and railway being cut, but the lake is open. He thinks he can make a shilling or two if he can get a cargo of wheat and bring it down the Shannon.'

'Well, nobody wants people to starve. Where would you join him?'

'He'll pick us up at Garrykennedy tomorrow morning.'

'Well, that's settled then,' said Mother.

Father turned to Dafydd. 'Have you ever been on a sailing barge?'

'No, I'd like that.'

*   *   *

The morning was hectic. Mother was frantically walking about giving orders and knitting, trying to finish a pair of socks she had on her needles for Father.

'I just don't understand how all the socks in the house could have disappeared,' she declared for the millionth time.

'Look, Mary, it doesn't matter if it's half an inch shorter than the other, just cast off and I'll wear it.'

'Typical man! It's not the top that will be short, you eejit, you'll have no toe!'

Katie was busy cutting sandwiches and trying to keep a straight face. She glanced at Dafydd who was sitting on a suitcase; he looked happy now that they were going. She looked at him with affection – he was really quite handsome. He must have sensed her attention because he glanced up. He'd been listening to the exchange about the socks too, and winked. She looked away quickly. Hooves were scraping in the yard as Peter backed Barney into the farm cart. Father came downstairs and dropped his old army kit bag on the floor.

'Katie, love, they have food in Wales, you know, and I'm only going for a fortnight!' She grinned at the mighty pile of sandwiches.

'We're out of stout,' she said regretfully. 'Mr Parry likes it – perhaps you'll get some on the way?' She wrapped the sandwiches in stiff brown paper, tied them with twine and crammed them into Father's grip.

'Well,' he said, 'let's get loaded up and away. Seamus, would you ever give a hand with the cases now?' Seamus shouldered the kit bag, dislodged Dafydd from his suitcase, and disappeared out into the yard. Mr Parry followed. Father came up to Mother as she was biting off the end of her wool, and spread his arms to give her a goodbye hug.

'You'll take care, won't you?' he said. 'You have Seamus back. I'll only –'

At that moment Mr Parry appeared in the door, 'Eamonn, I'm sorry to bother you but there's ... someone. There's an officer wants a word with you.'

'I'll just see what he wants, Mary,' Father said. 'It will be about the explosion the other night. Thank God it was nothing to do with us.'

Katie slipped around the table and into the shadow of the porch. Mr Parry came and stood beside her. She recognised the officer at once. He had got rid of the bandage on his hand and replaced it with sticking plaster. Beside her, Mr Parry said in a low voice, 'I explained to him that your father was badly shocked, he didn't seem to think there was anything to worry about.' Katie turned and smiled, 'Thank you,' she said.

But when she looked out into the yard, her smile froze on her face and a chill spread across her back. She couldn't see at once what was wrong; it reminded her of a scene from one of the plays in the village hall, a stage set – everyone trying to look natural, but not managing it at all. Soldiers were pacing about or standing, some looking at their boots, others up into the trees. They were busy looking casual, but Katie sensed that the real focus of attention was elsewhere. Where was it?

She scanned the yard. Father and the officer were talking, the officer laughing. Then she saw Seamus. He stood like the soldiers, acting, feigning casualness. Suddenly it was all horribly clear to Katie. The soldiers were after Seamus, and Seamus knew it. She followed the others into the yard. What was he thinking: Run for it? Stick it out? His head was still, but his eyes were alert. She willed him not to move. Those casually-held rifles in the soldiers' hands were ready. Now Father was walking back, smiling cheerfully.

'That's all right, everyone aboard. It's just routine, a quick run through the farm buildings and they'll be done. The

Sergeant will look after that, we've nothing to hide. Captain Delany would like a lift down in the cart with us. He wants to arrange the barge to get his men back to Nenagh.' Katie searched for the sergeant, to find that he was looking at Seamus just as a stoat stares down a rabbit. If they wanted Seamus, they had him, she thought. Why the search? Then, in a flash that actually hurt, she knew – Oh God ... the gun. Seamus's rifle. Was it still in the house?

She spun around to go back into the house; perhaps she could hide it? But suddenly there was a soldier where there had been no soldier before. He was standing, grinning, between her and the door.

'Say goodbye to Mr Parry and Dafydd, Katie,' called Father. 'We must be going.' She didn't even try to force a smile as Mr Parry reached down to shake her hand, then she turned to Dafydd, dismay etched on her face. But Dafydd was looking at Seamus. Then all at once he began to behave strangely. Scratching his head, he half-rose as if he'd forgotten something. Then he stood up and clasped his forehead. In a torrent of Welsh he began to clamber over the tailgate of the cart. Katie steadied him as he landed, but he pushed past her towards the house. He waved his arms at the astonished soldier, and still speaking Welsh ducked past him to disappear into the house like a rabbit.

'Don't worry,' shouted Mr Parry, laughing. 'He's forgotten his hurleys!' Katie heard the clatter of boots on the stairs. Then there was silence. What could he be doing? Had Marty given him one of his hurleys? Boots sounded on the stairs again and Dafydd appeared, carrying a loose bundle of sacking. A hurley stuck out from the top of it. Surely Marty hadn't given him both his sticks! Then, at last, Katie tumbled to what he was doing. How had she been so slow? She could sense rather than see the sergeant coming forward. Did he suspect anything? Dafydd had reached the cart. He'd need to pass the bundle up. Katie darted forward. Captain Delany was leaning out to take the bundle from Dafydd.

'I'll hold it for you,' she said, grabbing and nearly dropping it. It weighed a ton. The officer reached down and heaved Dafydd up. The sergeant was almost beside her now. No time to pass it up. She bent double and darted under the tail of the cart, then straightened up calling, 'Mr Parry!' With the appeal of desperation in her eyes, she thrust the bundle up at him. Then she jumped forward and gave Barney a slap on the backside.

'Gid up!' she yelled, and Barney moved forward towards the ramp. For one brief second she saw Mr Parry's astonished expression change to understanding as he pulled the bundle in, then he was gone.

She could hear the sergeant shouting at the officer to wait a minute, so she shouted Goodbye, then everyone was shouting and waving. For one last moment Katie caught Dafydd's eyes – they were dancing with excitement as he seemed to call out something special to her in Welsh. She blew him a kiss. The cart lurched up out of the yard and was gone. Between them they will get rid of it, slip it overboard from the barge perhaps, she thought with relief. Then she turned back to the yard and found a scene that had changed dramatically.

The sergeant was pushing Seamus over towards the barn. 'Hands against the wall and keep them there. Search him, soldier,' he snapped. 'Nobody goes into the house!'

'How dare you!' said Mother. 'You said the farm buildings.'

'Me?' sneered the Sergeant. 'No, not me!'

Katie went over to Mother and put an arm around her waist. Going as if to kiss her she whispered, 'Don't worry, Mother, the gun's gone, they can't accuse him without the gun.'

The search was thorough. Marty was hauled out of the byre, complaining bitterly that some people had work to do around here, and Katie could hear the thump of furniture being moved about in the house. She thought to herself, Bless you, Dafydd. Thanks to him there was nothing in the house for that beastly man to find. As the soldiers reappeared one by one, those guarding Seamus relaxed and allowed him to lower his hands. Several of them smiled at Katie as they emerged, and she felt that they were relieved too that nothing had been found. Cigarettes were lit and Katie was looking forward to showing her scorn to the sergeant when she heard his shrill cry of triumph. Everyone in the yard turned as one towards the house. Silence. What could he have found?

The sergeant appeared in the doorway and stood there enjoying his moment of triumph. He started to walk slowly, menacingly, towards Seamus. Then, for some reason, he seemed to change his mind and walked towards where Katie and Mother were standing. He stopped, smiling a thin-lipped smile, and held out his clenched fist. Slowly he opened his fingers. There, to Katie's horror, lay the metal clip which Seamus had so professionally flicked from the breach of his rifle as he had loaded it the day Kieran had arrived.

'Well?' the Sergeant demanded.

'I ... I don't know. What is it?' Mother was clearly perplexed.

Katie was thinking fast and said, 'I think it's something Dafydd picked up in the fields.'

It was as if the sergeant had been waiting for her to say this. He swung on her. 'Your poor little innocent Welsh boy?' he sneered. 'I wonder will that oaf of an officer ever have the wit to look at that boy's precious bundle? I doubt it. Hurleys ... hurleys, my foot.' He leaned towards Katie, so close that she could see his bad teeth. 'This, girlie, is all the evidence I need. You dodged me under the cart but your precious Seamus O'Brien won't. This is a real war, not some game played between so-called gentlemen. There is law, and there is order. But order comes first. You are now going to see how order works.'

He turned his back on her and rose on his toes like a cock on a dung heap and bellowed, 'Squad! Form up.' He strutted off, issuing orders as he went. 'Prisoner in the middle. You ... you ... and you: firing squad! By the left, quick march.'

It all happened so quickly – Seamus's pale, unseeing face in the centre of the squad of marching men, decent men, their faces questioning, dismayed but still marching. Katie gathered herself to run after them but Mother was swaying on her feet and needed her support. The soldiers were out of sight on the road. She eased Mother on to the block they used for chopping wood as further shouts and orders reached them. This couldn't be happening, it couldn't be real.

The three shots rang out almost as one. Rooks burst, cawing, from the trees. Katie abandoned Mother and dashed up towards the road. As she reached it a figure appeared, tottering above her. It was Seamus. She seized him and half-dragged, half-staggered with him down the slope into the yard, desperately inspecting him for wounds that were not there. He toppled against her.

'Sorry, Katie ... I must ... sit down. They fired over my head.' Then he was sick.

*   *   *

To begin with, Seamus talked and talked while Katie listened. It was like the old days with Father. First the firing squad, again and again, but now he wanted to talk about the night of the blast at the quarry.

'It was dark as sin before the explosion, Katie. We were spread out over the top of the quarry. We had it all set up, to move down quietly and trap the Free Staters as they tried to enter the quarry.'

'Why would they want to go in there?' Katie asked, trying to sound innocent.

'I'm not allowed to say,' said Seamus. Then, 'Oh what the hell, they'll never be dug out now. The guns and ammunition taken in Nenagh were hidden in the old cave.'

'But, Seamus, you knew it would kill Father if he found out!' Katie flared despite herself, but Seamus's face seemed to collapse and she regretted it at once. A furious nervous tick started below his right eye.

'I had no choice. Believe me, Katie, I tried. They thought Father's reputation was the best protection – the sparrow being safest under the hawk's nest,' he said ruefully. 'The quarry was walled up, everyone could testify that the cave was empty. Who would think of the cables as a way of getting stuff in and out?'

You left a Welsh boy out of your reckoning, Katie thought.

'Tell me about the explosion,' she said.

'I had just joined them from putting on my little act, moving lights about in the quarry yard. They had been hearing movements in the bushes above the quarry for some time. The Commandant was worried and said he would go down and have a look before we all moved down. It wasn't anybody, I'm sure, just the goats, remember the goats? We think the Commandant may have found the little house – the one we discovered years ago among the bushes and couldn't get into. It must have been the old powder store for the quarry.'

'Magazine,' corrected Katie, then bit her lip. But Seamus didn't notice.

'I don't know how he opened it. Perhaps he struck a match. What a bang! We were sure he'd be in bits. We rushed down the slope, and as we ran it seemed like there was another explosion – but it can't have been, it must just have been the moment when the rock gave way and slid into the pit. We met the goats charging away up the hill and thought they were the army! Thanks to the smell of the old Billy we didn't shoot them, nor each other either. The only light was where the bushes were on fire. It was amazing – the blast had ripped the Commandant's coat off him and thrown him into the bushes half-naked. The worst of his injuries came from where he got burned.'

'He's alive then?'

'Oh yes, Auntie Nora's looking after him, but he'll be out of action for a while.'

'What now? What about you?'

'I suppose they'll try to get him home, but I'm out of it, Katie.'

She looked up sharply. 'Out of it?'

'They don't want me. I was to hand in my rifle today. I suppose the army got it when they searched the house and that's why they pretended to execute me.'

'And good riddance to it,' said Katie, wondering what they might have done if they *had* found it. 'Why don't the Republicans want you?' she asked.

'They never found the informer – whoever it was gave the tip-off to the army: I think they suspect me. Uncle Mal stands up for me, and I think the Commandant would too but the others ... they think maybe I set a trap for them.'

'But the army nearly executed you!'

'It's no good, Katie. The Black and Tans used to do that just to protect their informers.'

'You, of all people, Seamus! I'm sorry.'

'You shouldn't be, Katie. I'm finished. I saw murder in that sergeant's eyes and I looked at death down the barrels of those three rifles. I'm not going to offer death to anyone again for any cause. We've got to find some other way.'

* * *

Weeks passed and Father was due home. His letters had been more and more cheerful as time went on and the notes Mr Parry had slipped in for Mother and Katie were reassuring. There were many things Katie wanted to keep to herself but, almost for the first time, she had begun to talk to Mother and was surprised at how easy it was. They worried about Seamus together and eventually, without saying anything to Seamus, Mother wrote to Mr Parry.

Katie was sitting in Dafydd's place on the shaft of the farm cart as a thin rain drifted across the yard when Seamus came out of the harness room and sat beside her. He pulled out a letter from an inside pocket.

'I got a letter from Mr Parry today. He could do with some help in the quarry over in Wales when Dad comes back. I think I might go over for a while, help him out.'

Katie managed to look surprised. 'I'll miss you.'

'No you won't. I'm not much company for anyone these days,' he said, and he rubbed at the ticking muscle below his eye. 'If you've any messages ... a letter for Dafydd maybe, I'll take it.'

That was a week ago and Katie had put off writing almost daily.

* * *

'Aren't you ready yet? You've had a week. It doesn't take that long to write a letter,' Seamus called up from the kitchen.

184

Katie put her head in her hands and groaned, then stared at the blank sheet in front of her. It was the last sheet in Mother's writing pad. It was this attempt or nothing. Crumpled up pieces of paper were scattered about her room.

Her problem had started when she had found the journal Dafydd was writing for his sister Megan, torn and buckled, where the sergeant had flung it as he stripped Dafydd's bed looking for guns. She had been furious as she gathered up the torn pages, tucking them in, taking care not to even glance at them. She would send the journal to him with a nice letter as soon as the post was back working. The journal lay in her top drawer with her handkerchiefs and no socks. But he'd never said it was private, she told herself. Still, she closed the drawer firmly. But then, he'd talked about being a journalist; perhaps it was a sort of newspaper article? She took it out. One of the pages had a boot print on it. She took a rubber and carefully removed what she could of the mark, but the writing was in pencil. Then finally she took the torn pages and pieced them together, sticking them with stamp paper. Seamus would take it tomorrow. She got brown paper and string ready to wrap it up. In the morning she would write her letter.

Katie woke in the middle of the night to a dream which had no form or shape only the lilt of Dafydd's Welsh accent. He had been talking to her; that's how it felt. She sat up in bed then and knew that she was going to read his journal. She struck a match. The flame of the candle rose, sank, and then rose again to a steady arrowpoint of light in the dark of her room, and she began to read.

The first pages were about Dafydd's journey through Dublin, and Katie was carried back to that first trip in the trap together. She stifled her chuckles at his description of the fleeing station master. Was she becoming jealous of Megan? It would be nice to have a brother to write to her like this. The next page caught her by surprise. 'Oh, Megan I'm in love (again! you say). She's like the rising sun, hair of spun gold. Driving her chariot ...' Katie blushed and half-closed the book. Ought she to be reading this? She hadn't known he felt like that about her ... but yet in a way she had. She was about to close the book virtuously when her eye caught an entry further down the page. '... my boots must come off too! My lovely quarry man's boots ... Oh Megan, the pain!' Poor Dafydd, and she'd been so horrid to him. That was their walk up to Uncle Mal's, what next? '... Risking life and limb, your reporter crept under the guns of the rebels,' (Josie and his shotgun) 'into the very heart of the rebel camp.'

As Katie read, the whole of that amazing week unfolded for her again, this time through Dafydd's eyes. She remembered whipping Barney into a gallop, 'Down from the mountain like a wolf on the fold she swept. Magnificent in war, hair flying, your hero rolling about on the floor of her chariot like a beetle on its back.' Katie wondered how she had ever thought she could stop the war on her own that time. Then Dafydd's writing changed, he was writing more slowly now, 'Secrets, Megan, are terrible things,' he wrote. 'She had never heard the story of how her Dad had forgotten his matches,' and Katie felt again the slap of Shannon waves against her feet.

The candle was burning low and Katie's eyes were pricking as she turned the last pages. She had been dreading reading of Kieran's arrival. 'Megan, I fear our Dafydd's time in the sun is over, a brighter light has come,' and she realised that Dafydd must have written that at the very moment when she was waving at him out the window to call Kieran back. Poor, noble Dafydd, did it hurt so much? She skimmed through a detailed description of how to blow up a mountain until the moment of the explosion and they were slipping and sliding down the waste together. 'At last my cup was full. There was I, clasped in her arms, her tears of gratitude wetting my cheek. The mountain of waste hurtling like the Gadarene swine into the abyss below when, all at once, sanity returned. All I wanted suddenly were Welsh hills, Welsh voices, our own valley and my black-eyed Megan.'

Katie let the copy-book slide to the floor and leant to blow out the candle. Relief and sadness mingled together but, as she closed her eyes, a voice within her murmured, 'Yes, that is how it was,' and she fell asleep.

*   *   *

'Come on, Katie! Father's train will be in in an hour, and I want to get my bags into the guard's room before he arrives.'

Katie thought of her discarded attempts: 'Dear Dafydd, I want to thank ...' crumple. 'My Dear Dafydd ...' crumple. How could she write! Of course he hadn't meant what he had written about her – those nice things – but suddenly he felt very close. He had been part of her life. She thought of him rolling about in the bottom of the trap. Or talking to her about Father beside the lake. Then there was the flash as the magazine blew up and she had thought him dead – then he was careering into her, all arms and legs, as the tip heaved under them. She thought of his fury when no-one would listen to him. She had loved him – not like Kieran – but as her Frog. He was a friend of all friends. She wanted to keep him, but not to hold him close because he didn't like that. She pulled the pad towards her for one last try. Almost absent-mindedly she began. This time the words came in an easy flow. After a bit she stopped to read over what she had written and laughed out loud. She had made a mistake, or was it a mistake? She stared at the page, smiling. She had begun her letter, *Dear Megan* ...

EPILOGUE

Oranmore stands at the head of Galway Bay, a few cottages and houses spreading out along the three roads which meet there: the road to Galway, the road to Dublin, and the road that runs down into County Clare. It was early summer, the civil war had petered out at last and too many young men had returned to too few farms. Two such young men stood now at the crossroads where the turf-smoke blew over them in scented wafts.

'If you can't make up your mind, toss for it. Heads, you come with me to Dublin and on to Liverpool where the streets are paved with gold. Tails, you take the road south to find hardship and poverty in the hills of Tipperary.'

'Can you toss with a sovereign?'

'It's well for you. I don't see why not.'

'It's all I've got,' said Kieran. He balanced the small gold coin on his thumbnail. 'Heads,' he called as the coin spun glinting in the sunlight before it fell into the dust of the road.

'Heads it is! Liverpool, here we come. Come on, Kieran, we'll take it by storm.'

'I think I'll go down through Clare just the same.'

'You can't do that! Go against the toss – that's the worst luck in the world.'

'Didn't it help me make up my mind? There's a glint of gold I have in mind that you won't find on the streets of Liverpool.'

'You had your mind made up long ago. Come on, give me the coin – it's bad luck to keep a coin once you go against the toss. You must give it away.'

'My sovereign! I'm not going against it at all. Amn't I just going to Liverpool the long way? I'll cross the Shannon at Killaloe and if success eludes me, I'll be off after you to Dublin and on the boat in no time.' Kieran picked up his bag. 'I'll make you a promise, though. If I do strike lucky and decide to stay there, I'll give the old sovereign away. How about that?'

'Fat lot of good that'll be to me.'

*　　*　　*

And that was how Mick-the-Shilling came to be known as Mick-the-Guinea, because he never spent the sovereign he'd been given, but carried it with him and showed it to everybody as the greatest treasure on earth.

A BRIEF HISTORY OF KATIE'S TIMES

When Katie would have been born in 1907, Ireland and England had been at loggerheads for over eight hundred years. Throughout this time, periods of peace had alternated with bloody rebellions during which the Irish tried to throw off English rule. These rebellions were followed by times of harsh repression. Irish lost their land to English and Scottish settlers, and penal laws denied Catholics their basic rights. By 1907, however, the earlier work of the great Irish peace-makers, Daniel O'Connell and Charles Stewart Parnell, had begun to bear fruit, and it seemed to be only a matter of time before England would give Ireland Home Rule. There were, however, many in Ireland who did not believe that Britain would ever give up their power. Members of the Irish Republican Brotherhood, the Fenians, were dedicated to armed rebellion.

In 1914, when Katie would have been seven, the promised Home Rule bill was about to be passed. At that moment however, Germany attacked Belgium, the First World War began, and Home Rule was, once again, put to one side. Many Irishmen felt that they should fight to defend Belgium, a small country like Ireland. During the war over 150,000 Irish volunteered, joining the British army. By the end of the war over 35,000 of these had been killed, and many more, like Father, had had their lives shattered.

While they were fighting, men such as Pádraic Pearse and James Connolly realised that England's preoccupation with the war was an opportunity for another Irish rebellion. Even if this wasn't successful, it would at least keep the flame of Irish nationalism alive. The Easter Rebellion of 1916, which took place when Katie would have been nine, was a military failure and might have done nothing for Irish nationalism had the English not executed fifteen of the Irish leaders. This set Irish nationalism ablaze.

In elections, which were held when the war was over in 1918, nationalist Sinn Féin swept to power. They effectively took over the government of the country and, for two and a half years, a guerrilla war (the War of Independence) was waged against the British. British troops in Ireland were augmented by specially tough recruits who came to be known as the Black and Tans because of the half-khaki, and half-black uniforms they wore. Even more hated were the Aux-iliaries, ex-army officers who were not only ruthless but clever as well.

Irish successes, and the bad behaviour of their own troops, swung

English public opinion against the war, and a truce was agreed. Negotiations between the British and Irish followed. At these, Michael Collins reluctantly signed a treaty which would make Ireland a Free State. But members of parliament would still have to swear an oath of allegiance to the king of England and the treaty did not extend to the six, mostly Protestant, counties of northern Ireland, so Ireland was partitioned.

The signing of the treaty split Irish nationalists. Eamon De Valera became the leader of the Republicans, who wished to go on fighting against England for a Republic which would include the six counties and which would require no oath to the king. Michael Collins knew that the Irish did not have the strength to defeat England, and became one of the leaders of the newly constituted Irish Free State. Matters came to a head when a group of Republicans took over the Four Courts in Dublin. The civil war started with the shelling of the Four Courts by Free State soldiers, the fighting which we have Dafydd hearing from Kingsbridge station.

The Irish civil war lasted for nearly a year. It was a bitter fight with both sides using tricks learned from the Black and Tans. Seamus's mock execution was a mild example. In the bitterness that followed, those Irish soldiers who had fought that even more terrible war in the trenches were forgotten.

LOCAL HISTORICAL DETAILS

Many of the incidents and places described in this book are real. Most of us have heard about the shelling of the Four Courts in Dublin. The Four Courts is still standing, but we cannot travel on the railway line which Dafydd and his father took from Westland Row to Kingsbridge (now Heuston) station, as it no longer exists. My inquisitive station master is imaginary but he is typical of many Dublin people who came out to watch the fighting as if it was a fireworks display.

Katie was looking forward to an extra long summer holiday because in 1922 the schools did close from 30 June to 25 September so that teachers could take Irish lessons. And the local school roof really did leak – one unfortunate girl had to leave her desk whenever there was a shower because the water came in on top of her!

The fighting in Nenagh, which the angry officer describes to Katie, started when a number of soldiers, stationed in the town, decided to support the Republican cause and took over the post office and other buildings. The Treaty soldiers then tried to turn them out. One Treaty officer, a Captain Byrne, was killed outside the Hibernian hotel, and an unfortunate bystander, Mrs O'Meara of O'Meara's hotel, who came out into the hotel porch to see what was happening, was also accidentally shot. There is no record of Seamus's guns being taken but it would have been a likely action.

It is difficult now to imagine a world without radio, but for nearly a week nobody outside Nenagh knew what was happening in the town. The Republicans had cut the telegraph wires, railway lines were torn up, and every road out of the town was either blocked with felled trees or had trenches dug across it. The town ran out of flour, and supplies had to be brought by barge down the Shannon. Despite the fighting there was a lot of good humour. Local people, even if they supported the Treaty, were very tolerant of the Republicans. John really did lose his hens, and the rhyme he found pinned to his door, is as reported in the *Nenagh Guardian*. But passions, particularly on the Republican side, ran very high. Seamus's outburst at dinner and Trench Coat's denouncement of Father are not exaggerated.

Welshmen have often helped in our mines and quarries. The name Griffith Parry belongs to a Welsh quarry man from Bangor who was buried in Castletown, near Portroe, in 1839. Quarrying stopped at the outbreak of the First World War, but started again once the civil war was over and continued on into the 1950s.

The story about the goats knowing when a rock-fall was about to occur is told locally; possibly the goats could feel the tip moving, just as Katie and Dafydd did. The quarries are fascinating, but they are also very dangerous: slate-falls are frequent and many have steep sides and deep water in them. Best to observe Father's warning: DANGER – KEEP OUT.

You will find the little harbour of Garrykennedy by turning down towards the lake at the village of Portroe. You won't find Katie's farm, but you will find many like it, gleaming with fresh whitewash, particularly after Easter. You can climb the steep road up from the quarries and imagine where Uncle Mal's farm might have been, or take the road through the Gap to the ancient stones known as the Graves of the Leinstermen.

Sadly, the possibility of finding an arms cache anywhere in Ireland still exists. If you do find anything suspicious do not touch it. Report it to the Guards and it will be destroyed.